The

Descriptions, Overused Words, and Taboos

By Kathy Steinemann

Print Edition

ISBN-13: 978-1544070186
ISBN-10: 1544070187

If you like this book, please remember to leave a review. Thanks!

Kathy

Table of Contents

Foreword

By Stuart Aken

The English language has a huge advantage over many others: it shamelessly steals, borrows, modifies, and combines words from other languages. As a result, it is rich in variety. The language allows users to express any given idea in diverse ways.

Writers in English, whether creating fiction, composing poetry, or recording facts, have multiple opportunities to vary their means of articulating their thoughts. And, when authors use synonyms to effect, they not only enliven their work but simultaneously provide the prospect for readers to increase their vocabularies. A win/win situation if ever there was.

Any decent thesaurus lists alternatives for the word a writer seeks. But it takes experience and imagination to provide suggestions for replacements that will bring life to a piece of writing. Examples of usage, samples of extremes, instances of subtlety, and variations in mood and tone all feature in Kathy Steinemann's excellent resource. She gives readers of this book comprehensive lists of similar or related words to those commonly used, providing real substitutes for the conventional and allowing writers to construct work that employs the most pertinent words wherever possible.

Using this source, a writer can be certain that her characters will merely cry no more. They may weep, wail, moan, caterwaul, pine, snivel, yowl, or any of dozens of other emotive actions. But they won't be forced simply to cry. And, using Kathy's examples as a lead, authors can improve their writing and raise it above the crowd,

1

allowing readers to fully immerse themselves in the resulting creations.

—

Stuart Aken is a novelist, storyteller, blogger, and developing poet. Refusing to be bound by genre, he often mixes styles and content to produce unique works of fiction that capture the imagination whilst purveying captivating messages about the human condition. He has produced romance, thriller, epic fantasy, science fiction, and other works, which stretch the normal boundaries of their allotted category. You'll find his work, along with informative pieces on language use, opinions, and personal insights on his website at StuartAken.net.

Why I Wrote This Book

During my writing endeavors I often found myself creating alternatives for overused words. I saved those word lists in a manual on my computer and developed many into blog posts.

Several of my blog followers urged me to publish the lists. I expanded them to produce this book.

As you write, realize that you won't find every word you need in a thesaurus. For instance, a search of my favorite thesauri for *go* didn't show *skirr*, which means "to move rapidly, especially with a whirring sound."

When not writing, pay attention as you read or do crossword puzzles. You'll encounter alternatives that don't appear in your usual sources.

By the way, sprinkled throughout these chapters you'll find ideas for story prompts. Snap 'em up at will.

Overused Words and Phrases

This section covers nuisances that annoy writers around the globe.

You know what I'm talking about, don't you? Those *little* pests that cause *big* problems, creeping into prose and poetry like a virus. You insert a favorite phrase. It seems so right that you insert it a few more times.

Great.

Until you realize you've repeated it ad nauseam.

No worries. Even if you don't find a substitute phrase in these pages, you'll learn how to engage your ingenuity and create alternatives.

Although you'll encounter a few "rules" in this book, writing is not rules. It is a fusion of emotions, senses, and conflict. Whatever engages your readers should be the rule.

Common Pitfalls

Check your writing for the following and handle them with care. I've included many in the lists throughout this book.

<u>A</u>
About, absolutely, almost, amazing, are, assume, awesome

<u>B</u>
Bad, basically, be, be able to, beautiful, been, begin, being, believe, big, bring

<u>C</u>
Can, clear the throat

<u>D</u>
Decide

<u>E</u>
Essentially, even, exciting, experience, extremely

<u>F</u>
Fast, feel, feel like, frown

<u>G</u>
Get, go, good, great

<u>H</u>
Have, hear, honestly

<u>I</u>
I, imagine, incredible, incredibly, interesting, is

<u>K</u>
Know

<u>L</u>
Laugh, like, literally, little, look, loud

N
Nauseated, nauseous, nice, nod, noisy, note, notice

O
Only

P
Pleasant

Q
Quick, quite

R
Realize, really, remember

S
Said, say, scowl, see, seem, shrug, sigh, sit, small, smile, sound, sound like, start

T
Taste, that, then, think, totally, touch, try

U
Unbelievable, unique, use

V
Very

W
Want, was, watch, went, were, wonder

Beautiful

***Beautiful* often ends up ugly.**

Too many instances of any word in your prose or poetry will dilute its effectiveness, especially if readers consider that word stale or stereotypical.

You look so <u>beautiful</u>, darling.

This is a <u>beautiful</u> meal, chef.

What a <u>beautiful</u> day!

The rainbow is <u>beautiful</u>.

Look at that <u>beautiful</u> woman.

This dress is <u>beautiful</u>.

If you resort to *beautiful* more than a handful of times throughout a novel, dialogue excluded, your writing will suffer.

At the end of this chapter, you'll find alternatives for *beautiful*. Rather than plug in substitutions, try exploiting the suggestions as catalysts to transform the words into verbs or nouns.

Consider this sentence:

Helen was <u>beautiful</u>.

Let's pick a few words from the list and do a rewrite.

Helen's <u>ethereal</u> <u>poise</u> <u>tantalized</u> every suitor who bowed the knee before her.

Better?

Cultivate your creativity.

Instead of searching for overused descriptors, consulting a thesaurus, and selecting substitutions, try capitalizing on your finds and transforming them into verbs or nouns.

Can we improve on this sentence?

Every man Sonja met thought she was <u>beautiful</u>.

Time for a rewrite.

Sonja's compelling charm captivated every man she met.

Although the sentence is more *tell* than *show*, it is stronger than the first version.

What do you think of this humdrum statement?

Tasha's eyes looked <u>beautiful</u> in the starlight.

Anyone could write that, including my eight-ear-old nephew. What can we do with three more adjectives from the list?

The <u>ethereal</u> <u>radiance</u> of the stars couldn't match the <u>allure</u> of Tasha's eyes.

Now we have a narrator who shows Tasha's beauty and possibly his attraction or infatuation.

Here's another mundane sentence:

The water looked <u>beautiful</u>.

Says who?

To a scuba diver, it could mean an ocean with almost limitless visibility. A painter or photographer might admire a scene of sparkling ripples and diving seagulls. An angler could see beauty in water filled with fish.

Remember who your protagonists or narrators are and choose creative words to match their personalities and backgrounds.

How can we improve on _beautiful water_ using suggestions from the list?

The diver gazed into the mesmerizing deep, intoxicated by its boundless visibility.

During the magical moments when day meets night, the artist captured on canvas the diving seagulls, sparkling waves, and pristine reef.

Glittering schools of fish darted to and fro, hypnotizing the fishermen with their promise of a delectable dinner.

Consider a science fiction story featuring a beautiful robot. Who thinks she's beautiful? Another robot? A human? Or maybe a dog? Point of view (POV) makes a huge difference, and you can reflect that POV in the words you choose.

For instance, here's a boring sentence that describes a housekeeping bot:

ZylTrann was beautiful.

Let's examine that perception through the internal monologue of three different protagonists.

A butler robot might summon these descriptors from his memory banks:

ZylTrann's superior intelligence and extraordinary computing speed have surpassed all expectations of the Masters. Surely that will save her from my inglorious fate with the Recyc—

We can assume from the interrupted thought that ZylTrann's associate just met his demise with the Recycler Corps.

Perhaps genetically engineered Rover feels intimidated by ZylTrann and regards her in a negative way. His canine mind devises dog parallels:

Nothing fazes that formidable bucket of bolts. Stupid bot won't even short out when I pee on her leg. Zapped me real good. Why don't the Masters get rid of her?

Poor Rover! He had to learn the hard way that ZylTrann doesn't appreciate being used like a fire hydrant.

A human would express different thoughts from those of our other two protagonists.

Foolish Zyltrann thinks her <u>remarkable</u> computational skills will save her from the Recycler Corps, but nothing beats the new <u>eroto</u>-bots with their <u>seduction</u> functions.

Note the assignment of gender to the human-made beings. Another writer might prefer to use *it*. Reader involvement and expectations would then change.

Soar beyond the limits.

Lewis Carroll invented adjectives such as *slithy* (*slimy + lithe*), *frabjous* (*fabulous + joyous*), and *mimsy* (*miserable + flimsy*). Try a similar approach with suffixes.

<u>al</u>: pertaining to
<u>esque</u>: resembling, reminiscent of
<u>ful</u>: full of
<u>ic, ical</u>: pertaining to
<u>ious, ous</u>: quality, nature
<u>ine</u>: relating to
<u>ish</u>: having the quality of
<u>ive</u>: tending to, having the nature of
<u>licious</u>: delightful, extremely attractive
<u>like</u>: like
<u>ly, y</u>: characterized by, like
<u>ous</u>: full of
<u>ular</u>: relating to, resembling

Transform nouns into descriptors like *rainbowesque, pantherine,* and *butterfly-like.*

Let's assume you're writing a fantasy novel in which the heroine is a stunningly beautiful woman named Lyrrical. Synonyms for *beautiful* in your world could be *lyrricalesque, lyrricallicious,* or *lyrricaline.*

In another story, someone might be *swan-like* or *peacockish*. Both terms, while suggesting attractiveness, present a different personality. We consider swans as serene, but a peacock might be the epitome of vanity.

Choose carefully, and you'll show your characters' personalities without excessive description.

Harness stereotypes.

You could liken a beautiful nurse to a curvaceous android.

We expect machine intelligences to be emotionless but efficient. Identification of the woman as a nurse paints a stereotypical picture of her clothing, including shoes with noiseless soles.

Just three words, *curvaceous*, *android*, and *nurse*, create a mini-portrait.

Incidentally, if you decide to compare your protagonist to a celebrity, the celeb should be familiar to the majority of your readers. Do you know who Emilia Clarke is? She plays gorgeous Daenerys Targaryen, Mother of Dragons on *Game of Thrones*. I'm a *Game of Thrones* fan, but I didn't know her real name until I investigated.

Manipulate stereotypes and give them an unexpected twist.

How about a breathtaking psychiatrist who believes she's ugly, and who self-medicates until the effects of the drugs *do* render her ugly?

Perhaps you introduce a glamorous movie star who wears false ... everything ... and appears in multiple tabloids after a paparazzo catches her at her worst. Then we learn she's suffering from a rare disease that has made her hairless and skinny, with blotched skin.

Or imagine a beautician who spends her after-work hours in holey sweatpants and mustard-stained T-shirts while awaiting assignments for her real job as an assassin. You could give that surprise compelling impact with an imaginative choice of adjectives and adverbs.

Play with character flaws.

A person might appear picture perfect but possess underlying qualities that aren't quite so appealing. Combine negatives with positives to create fresh nuances of character. You'll soon discover imaginative phrases such as:

- Aloof radiance
- Ambiguous poise
- Awkward grace
- Cold charm
- Dark splendor
- Detached attractiveness
- Flawed perfection
- Hollow magnetism
- Icy allure
- Indifferent appeal
- Intimidating refinement
- Misleading flirtatiousness
- Remote majesty
- Reserved beauty
- Saccharine sweetness
- Snobbish elegance
- Snooty charisma
- Tainted loveliness
- Unapproachable glamor

Are you ready to exercise your creativity? Here's the list.

<u>A</u>
Adorable, alluring, amazing, angelic, appealing, arresting, astonishing, astounding, attractive, awe-inspiring, awesome

<u>B</u>
Beauteous, bedazzling, beguiling, bewitching, bodacious, bonny, boundless, breathtaking

<u>C</u>
Captivating, celestial, charismatic, charming, chaste, cherubic, come-hither, comely, compelling, consummate, coquettish, cosmopolitan, curvaceous, cute

D
Dazzling, delectable, delicious, delightful, desirable, disarming, divine, dreamy, dumbfounding, dynamic, dynamite

E
Electrifying, elegant, empyrean, enchanting, endearing, engaging, enrapturing, enthralling, enticing, entrancing, ethereal, exceptional, exciting, exotic, exquisite, extraordinary, eye-catching

F
Fabulous, fair, fascinating, fetching, fiery, fine, flabbergasting, flaming, flawless, flirtatious, formidable, foxy

G
Genteel, genuine, glamorous, glittering, glorious, glowing, good-looking, gorgeous, gracious, gripping

H
Handsome, heady, heavenly, hot, hypnotic

I
Immeasurable, impeccable, imposing, incomparable, inconceivable, incredible, indescribable, inescapable, inexorable, infinite, inimitable, intoxicating, intriguing, inviting, irresistible

J
Jaw-dropping

K
Knockout

L
Limitless, lissome, lovely, luminous, luscious, lush, lustrous

M
Magical, magnetic, magnificent, majestic, matchless, measureless, mesmerizing, mind-boggling, momentous, mouth-watering, mysterious, mystical

N
Noble, nonpareil

O
Opulent, otherworldly, outstanding, overpowering, overwhelming

P
Paralyzing, peerless, perfect, perky, personable, phenomenal, picture-perfect, picturesque, pleasing, poised, polished, potent, prepossessing, pretty, pristine, provocative, pulchritudinous, pure

R
Radiant, rapturous, rare, ravishing, recherché, red-hot, refined, regal, remarkable, resplendent, riveting

S
Saintly, salacious, scorching, seductive, sensational, sensuous, seraphic, serene, singular, slinky, smoking, sophisticated, sparkling, spectacular, spectral, spellbinding, spine-tingling, splendid, splendiferous, splendorous, staggering, stately, statuesque, striking, stunning, stupefying, stylish, sublime, sui generis, sultry, sunny, superior, supreme, surreal, sweet

T
Taking, tantalizing, teasing, tempting, thrilling, titillating, torrid, transcendent, transcendental, transfixing

U
Unbelievable, uncanny, unearthly, unequalled, unimaginable, unique, unprecedented, unrivaled, unsurpassed, untold

V
Vivacious, voluptuous

W
Wholesome, willowy, winning, winsome, wondrous

Big

Another *big* problem for writers: overuse of *big*.

If you search Google for "most overused words in writing," *big* will appear on the majority of lists you find. This chapter provides more than one hundred alternatives.

Workarounds can add character to your writing.

Compare the following sets of sentences.

Bernard's ego was <u>bigger</u> than his bank account.

Bernard's ego outmatched his <u>mammoth</u> bank account.

Readers could misunderstand the first sentence. Although they might assume Bernard has a big bank account, the second sentence leaves no doubt and replaces *was* with a more active verb.

The <u>big</u> tiger moved silently through the grass.

The <u>behemoth</u> tiger stalked silently through the grass.

The second example replaces *big* with *behemoth*, an appropriate description for a large tiger. A more active verb completes the transformation.

The <u>big</u> bruise on Sylvia's arm was obvious, even under several layers of makeup.

Sylvia couldn't conceal the <u>monstrous</u> bruise on her arm, no matter how much makeup she slathered over it.

In the second sentence, *monstrous* leaves no doubt about the size of the bruise. Why does Sylvia try to conceal it? Did you notice the removal of *was*?

"Give me the <u>biggest</u> suitcase," Mya said. "I'll be gone for eight days."

"Give me the <u>jumbo</u> suitcase," Mya said. "I'll be gone for eight days."

In this scenario, *jumbo* seems the perfect adjective.

A big crowd showed up for the inauguration, although not as big as many had expected.

An appreciable crowd showed up for the inauguration, although not as humongous as many had hoped.

The above presents a prime example of how subtle word choices can alter the feel of a sentence.

The dentist looked into my mouth. "That's a big cavity you've got there, Stefania."

The dentist peered into my mouth. "That's an enormous cavity you've got there, Stefania."

Enormous implies a cavity that might require dental work such as a crown, extraction, or root canal. Other descriptors like *considerable* or *substantial* would provide less dramatic pictures.

Show size.

Without relying on any adjectives from the list at the end of this chapter, we can still show *big*.

I had a big crush on the deliveryman.

Every time the deliveryman knocked on the door, my pulse raced and my cheeks flamed.

The second sentence provides a classic specimen of *tell* converted to *show*.

The big story of the day's entertainment news was the divorce of Angelina Jolie and Brad Pitt.

The divorce of Angelina Jolie and Brad Pitt dominated the day's entertainment news.

The second sentence provides another removal of *was* and eliminates the size descriptor.

My <u>big</u> worry is that my hair will turn grey before I reach forty. I already see wiry white strands.

Whenever I spot another wiry white strand, I panic. Will my hair turn grey before I reach forty?

The first paragraph illustrates classic *tell*. The second *shows*, with *panic* replacing *big worry*. We see a narrator who might be overdramatic or narcissistic.

Try word combinations with *-sized* to show largeness.

A <u>cockroach-sized</u> red ant bit my ankle.

Every night two <u>cougar-sized</u> alley cats roamed the neighborhood, searching for rodents.

<u>Boulder-sized</u> mushrooms squished underfoot as the hunter crept through the forest.

A deluge of <u>egg-sized</u> raindrops drenched the ground within seconds.

<u>Saucer-sized</u> green eyes glowed from every crevice in the cave.

Have you chosen the appropriate connotation?

Perhaps *big* is the wrong nuance.

Big footfalls might be better as *ponderous* footfalls.

Does your WIP describe a *big* crisis that affects everyone in a city? You could change it to a *citywide* crisis. Likewise for countries: *countrywide* crisis. The entire Earth? Try *worldwide* or *global.*

You could label Tim's *big* impetus as his *overarching* impetus.

Better alternatives for Brandon's *big desire* might be Brandon's *yearning* or Brandon's *obsession.*

Ready for a few exercises?

Rewrite the following, editing out all forms of *big*. Use at will as story prompts.

1. A big storm blew in from the north, pelting the street with big hailstones. The projectiles smashed windows, dented cars, and decimated trees.

I scrambled into a big garbage bin behind the pharmacy and listened to nature's big bullets beating on the metal. When I reached to massage a cramp in my left toe, my fingers dipped into something smelly and slimy.

I puked. [Why does the narrator puke? Because of the smell? Because he recognizes the slimy material? Because he's allergic to something in the garbage bin?]

2. Nobody knew Phil's big secret. Except me. The big burden haunted me day and night. Every time I closed my eyes, even to blink, I could see the big horror of what he had done. He had me to lean on, but I had no one. How could I live with this knowledge?

3. Fourteen days until the big event. Fourteen days of planning and pacing and worrying. Could I pull it off? It would be a big challenge, one I planned to meet.

But you know what they say about the plans of mice and men.

4. "Excuse me, everyone," said the boss, "I have a big announcement to make. Starting today, you will all be eligible for big bonuses if you [Insert humorous or horrendous activity that workers must perform to earn those bonuses.]"

5. Anderson Carter, *5 O'Clock National News* anchor, adjusted his tie. "We have big news breaking from the White House this hour." He scrutinized the paper that someone off camera had just handed him. "This can't be right."

His puzzled expression deepened as he tapped his earbud. "You're sure?" He stared into the camera. "Big news, really big news. And remember, you heard it here first. According to reputable sources, [Insert something topical. Can you make it funny? Unbelievable? Horrible?]"

6. Ruby maintained a big garden filled with a big assortment of vegetables, berries, and fruits. Every morning she strolled through the rows, her big skirts brushing big drops of dew off the leaves as she swished by. Each stroll led her to a well-groomed pansy bed <u>big</u> enough to be an adult grave.

She would stand, hands folded below her waist, with a <u>big</u> enigmatic smile on her face. Sometimes I heard her murmur. I could never quite make out what she said, but it sounded grim. What had Ruby buried under those pansies?

I decided to sneak into her garden that night with my garden trowel.

7. A <u>big</u> flash of blinding brilliance assaulted Trystan's beady eyes. Shortly thereafter, a <u>big</u> boom resonated from the <u>big</u> cliffs across the canyon. He stumbled back a step. <u>Big</u> boulders and jagged rocks pelted the earth a few paces away. He grabbed his dead squire's shield and raised it to protect his head.

No need.

The boulders transmutated into a gentle rain of flower petals. Every hair on Trystan's body bristled, invigorated by an energy that could mean only one thing.

Magic was not dead.

Direct replacements for *big*.

You'll find a few of the following *big* alternatives sprinkled throughout this chapter. Pay attention to nuances. *Ample* does not provide the same impact as *titanic*.

<u>#</u>
2XL, 3XL

<u>A</u>
Ample, appreciable, astronomical

<u>B</u>
Ballooned, bear-sized, behemoth, beyond-measure, bloated, boundless, broad, Brobdingnagian, bulky

<u>C</u>
Capacious, chunky, citywide, countrywide, colossal, commodious, considerable, cosmic, cyclopean

D
Daunting, decuman, distended

E
Elephantine, enormous, epic, Everestine, extensive, extra-large

F
Far ranging, formidable

G
Galactic, galaxy-wide, gargantuan, generous, giant, giant-sized, gigantic, gigantiform, ginormous, global, Goliath, goodly, grand, great, grizzlyesque

H
Hefty, Herculean, honking, huge, hulking, humongous

I
Immane (archaic), immeasurable, immense, imposing, incalculable, inescapable, inestimable, infinite, inflated, inordinate, international

J
Jabba-the-Hutt-huge, jumbo, Jupiteresque

K
King-sized, Kodiak-sized

L
Large, leviathan, limitless, lofty

M
Macroscopic, mammoth, massive, maxi, measureless, mega, mighty, mondo, monolithic, monstrous, monumental, mountainous, muckle

N
Never-ending

O
Olympian, outsized, overlarge, oversized

<u>P</u>
Pervasive, prodigious

<u>Q</u>
Queen-sized

<u>R</u>
Rhinoesque

<u>S</u>
Sasquatchesque, sizable, skyscraperesque, staggering, stupendous, substantial, super-sized, swollen

<u>T</u>
Thumping, titanic, towering, tremendous

<u>U</u>
Ubergross, ubiquitous, ultra-large, unbounded, universal, untold

<u>V</u>
Vast, voluminous

<u>W</u>
Walloping, wall-to-wall, whacking, whale-sized, whopping, wide, worldwide

<u>X</u>
XL, XXL, XXXL

Bring

How often do you depend on *bring, brings, brought,* and *bringing*?

Let's review the Dictionary.com definition of *bring*: "to carry, convey, conduct, or cause (someone or something) to come with, to, or toward the speaker."

It's an easy word to replace.

"<u>Bring</u> me the stick, Buddy," said the Yorkie's owner.

"<u>Fetch</u> me the stick, Buddy," said the Yorkie's owner.

Fetch is a common command given by owners to dogs, and it's more appropriate in this situation than *bring*.

The courier said he would <u>bring</u> the package before 5 p.m.

The courier said he would <u>deliver</u> the package before 5 p.m.

When you think of a courier, doesn't *deliver* evoke a better image than *bring*?

Walter <u>brought</u> his daughter to the picnic.

Walter <u>piggybacked</u> his daughter to the picnic.

Walter could have *driven* his daughter to the picnic, but *piggybacked* shows a happy interaction that will engage readers.

The driver <u>brought</u> the bride to the wedding in a stretch limo.

The driver <u>chauffeured</u> the bride to the wedding in a stretch limo.

Chauffeured + limo = perfect match.

"Be sure to <u>bring</u> a warm coat," Mom said. "It's freezing outside."

"Be sure to <u>wear</u> a warm coat," Mom said. "It's freezing outside.

Besides replacing *bring* with a more appropriate verb, *wear* provides alliteration, an engaging technique when applied with caution.

Dennis always brought a pile of paperwork with him to our lunch dates.

Dennis always lugged a pile of paperwork with him to our lunch dates.

Do you think Dennis realizes the lunch engagements are dates? Maybe he needs a slap upside the head. *Lugged* implies a heavy pile of paperwork.

Robyn grabbed her coat. "Bring me home. Now. I've had enough of your lies."

Robyn grabbed her coat. "Drive me home. Now. I've had enough of your lies."

A simple verb change provides detail without adding to word count.

The wizened man brought me to the island in a dory.

The wizened man rowed me to the island in a dory.

Since a dory is a small boat, *rowed* reinforces the visual. Although motors propel some dories, most operate on oar-power.

Exercises and story prompts.

Before you revise your WIP, try these exercises. Edit out all forms of *bring*. Massage at will for story prompts.

1. "I'll never bring Bertram to another company picnic," said Mary. "He ate all the chili then started a farting contest with everyone in Accounting."

"That's not so bad," Danielle answered. "My date sat on the lasagna I brought. Then he peeled it off his butt and ate it!"

2. Three times every solar year, *Venture IV* brought a fresh supply of honey-garlic barbecue sauce to Asteroid Anastasia. The Vortonese couldn't get enough of the stuff. Their alien biology converted the sauce into excrement of pure saffinirium, the most efficient power source in the galaxy.

3. Leon scuffed up dust as he searched the roadside for bottles. Every night he <u>brought</u> a sackful to the recycle depot and collected his paltry take.

But today wasn't like every other day. A glimmer in the ditch caught his attention. He stooped to scrape the gravel off what turned out to be a coin with strange glyphs circling the silhouette of a unicorn.

He <u>brought</u> it close to his wondering eyes for a thorough inspection, and rubbed it to a soft shine.

A dust devil swirled around him. The trees disintegrated, reforming into jagged shapes that jutted into a green-tinged sky with triple moons.

His eyes bulged. "What the—"

4. Tabitha <u>brought</u> me a mouse and dropped it at my feet. Even from my six-foot-two height, I could hear her proud purring.

"What did you <u>bring</u> me, kitty-cat? Another present?" With a grimace, I crouched to retrieve it. The miniscule creature was still warm. "Damn!" This was no mouse. Smaller ears. Bushy tail. It could have passed for a miniature squirrel.

The creature twitched as I turned it over to study its abdomen. Its eyes flickered open, and a thin voice squeaked, "<u>Bring</u> me to your leader, human."

5. "I'll <u>bring</u> you roses and chocolates," crooned Josh as he twirled Alvina around the damp basement, "and diamonds too. 'Cause I know I'll never find another woman like you." He dipped her, <u>brought</u> her back up, and kissed her on the forehead.

"Well," she said as she stomped her stiletto heels, "I'd be more likely to believe that if you <u>brought</u> me [Insert something scary or funny. Is Alvina a kidnap victim playing a part to avoid being murdered? A disgruntled girlfriend? Josh's mother? A hallucination?]"

6. Paisley extended her chubby fists. "Here, Daddy. I <u>brought</u> this just for you."

Howard's eyes widened. He <u>brought</u> one palm to his left shoulder and collapsed onto the floor.

7. A searing sun scalded the landscape, <u>bringing</u> death to everything it touched. *Roamer-538* hummed through dead trees and under rocky crags, keeping to shadows wherever possible.

Anatole scanned the cockpit readouts. Even with environmental controls <u>brought</u> down to maximum cool, the in-ship temperature had climbed beyond comfort levels.

Stumped for *bring* alternatives? Check this list.

Each word provides a different nuance. Choose carefully or exploit the words as idea generators.

<u>A</u>
Assist

<u>B</u>
Backpack, bear

<u>C</u>
Carry, cart, chauffeur, come across with, come up with, contribute, convey, cough up

<u>D</u>
Deliver, dispatch, donate, drag, draw, drive

<u>E</u>
Escort, expedite

<u>F</u>
Fast-track, ferry, fetch, fork out, fork over, fork up, forward, furnish

<u>G</u>
Guide

H
Hand over, haul, heave, heft, hump

L
Lead, lug

M
Mail, motor, move

O
Oar

P
Pack along, piggyback, pilot, portage, post, provide, pull

R
Relay, relocate, row

S
Schlepp, scrape up, shell out, ship, shoulder, steer, supply

T
Take, take along, take with, tote, traject, transfer, transmit, transport, truck, tug, turn over

W
Walk, wear

Clear the Throat

Irritating in real life, ditto in fiction.

Have you ever shared space with someone who clears their throat every few minutes?

Annoying.

The first few times, you try to ignore the habit. Then it begins to wear on your nerves. You feel like grabbing a pillow and putting a permanent end to the irritation.

Fictional characters who clear their throats too often will annoy readers too.

Determine motivations.

The following emotions are only a few that could incite a throat-clearing episode:

Agitation, anxiety, apprehension, concern, deviousness, distraction, distrust, doubt, embarrassment, fear, guilt, insecurity, love, nervousness, skepticism, uncertainty, unease

Consider substituting body language for each of these emotions.

Agitation
Pacing
Nail biting
Forced laughter
Fidgeting with hair or clothing

Anxiety
Jerky movements
Trembling hands
Grinding teeth
Rapid, shallow breathing

Apprehension
Pursed lips
Audible breathing
Tugging on an ear
Scratching a non-existent itch

Concern
Pale face
Visible sweating
Wringing hands
Fidgeting or jiggling keys, cell phone, or jewelry

Deviousness
Rapid blinking
Lack of eye contact
Uncharacteristic stuttering
Gnawing on inside of cheek

Distraction
Rubbing arms
Clenching fists
Adjusting clothing
Audible exhalations

Distrust
Cocked head
Interlocking fingers
Clasping hands behind back
Abbreviated greeting or handshake

Doubt
Squinting
Chin tilted upward
Scratching the neck
Rubbing or touching the nose

Embarrassment
Shuffling feet
Flushed cheeks
Coughing or stuttering
Covering face with hands

Fear
Flared nostrils
Furrowed brow
Rocking on heels
Tightly clenched mouth

Guilt
Cracking voice
Trembling chin
Tugging at collar or clothing
Staring at the floor or one's toes

Insecurity
Hugging oneself
Tight-lipped smile
Fiddling with hair or makeup
Shifting weight from foot to foot

Love
Licking one's lips
Flawless personal grooming
Smiling for no apparent reason
Constant talking to others about one's love interest

Nervousness
Unable to sit or stand still
Unable to focus on conversation
Tapping feet or drumming fingers
Handbag or briefcase held in front of body

Skepticism
Smirking
Cocking the head
Wrinkling the nose
Narrowing the eyes

Uncertainty
Biting on nails or lips
Twiddling thumbs
Holding steepled fingers to lips
Glancing away during conversation

Unease
Insomnia
Trembling
Tense muscles
Inability to concentrate

A few more alternatives for *clear the throat* include:

Agonize, babble, blanch, blush, bow the head, brood, care, carp, chafe, disbelieve, dread, fib, flinch, flounder, freeze, fret, fume, fuss, gape, gob, grin, hawk, hem and haw, huff, hum, hyperventilate, leer, lie, mistrust, mope, mumble, ogle, panic, perspire, pray, question, quiver, redden, regret, rue, seethe, shake, show alarm, slouch, slump, spit, squirm, stammer, stew, swelter, tremble, turn red, twitch, worry, wriggle writhe

Careful. Some alternatives will *tell* rather than *show*.

Let's review a few practical applications.

Lester cleared his throat and said, "I don't want to go."

His mother responded, "What did you say?"

Lester spoke so quietly or indistinctly that his mother didn't hear or understand him. We can make that clear.

Lester mumbled, "I don't want to go."

His mother responded, "What did you say?"

Better, and we cut the word count by four.

Emily cleared her throat. "He's ten minutes late. Why can't he ever show up on time?"

Given the situation, we can assume Emily is agitated.

Emily paced. "He's ten minutes late. Why can't he ever show up on time?"

Now a cardboard Emily turns into a real character who moves in our imagination, and we see her motivation.

"I don't believe that," Trudy said. She <u>cleared her throat</u>. "All the way to Mars and back in less than six months? Impossible."

Trudy's motivation? Skepticism.

"I don't believe that." Trudy smirked. "All the way to Mars and back in less than six months? Impossible."

The revised version eliminates the dialogue tag and shows us a skeptical Trudy, accomplished with four fewer words.

"I didn't mean to, really, I didn't." Francine <u>cleared her throat</u>. "How can I make it up to you?"

Francine feels guilty about something. Can we demonstrate that with something besides a noise in her throat?

"I didn't mean to, really, I didn't." Francine stared at her toes. "How can I make it up to you?"

If you don't see what you need here, determine your character's motivation and then check the internet for alternatives.

For example, a search for *"body language" guilt* produces several excellent results.

Ready for some exercises and story prompts?

Replace all instances of throat clearing in the following. Like an idea? Use it.

1. "Well, it's like this, see," Morris said to the airport security officer. He glanced at the other passengers in line and then <u>cleared his throat</u>. "I stopped to help an old lady. She must have stole my boarding pass. I gotta get on that plane. Please." [Morris seems to be lying. Can you show that with body language? Or maybe he's telling the truth about the old lady and has a compelling reason to board the flight.]

2. The professor scanned the bored faces in the lecture room. He <u>cleared his throat</u>. "What if all the coincidences in our lives were really caused by aliens with a hidden agenda? What if we found out? How would we feel?"

A student near the back flinched, and his face blanched. [Is the student an alien? That blanching face seems suspicious. Maybe he's part of a top-secret organization tasked with hunting down aliens, and he thinks the professor is one.]

3. Sister Ashanti stared at the photo of the cancer-ridden man on her Facebook timeline. Tears filled her eyes. *So skinny.* Could she do it? Just once more? She <u>cleared her throat</u> and placed her palm over the photo. [What happens next? Does she pray for the man? If so, does his cancer disappear? Is the man related to her? Someone who wronged her? Maybe she curses him.]

4. "My wife has a real green thumb," Arnold said to the florist, "but the plants she buys from the grocery store are always filled with soil gnats." He <u>cleared his throat</u> and pointed to a Swedish ivy in the window. "That one looks nice, but I don't want to bring anything home unless it's pest free."

"No worry." The florist smiled. "You won't find any bugs on my plants." [Why? Is this truly a Swedish ivy, or is it a sentient creature from another planet? Does the florist fertilize the plants with something funny? Horrific? Rather than *have* bugs, could the plant *be* a bug?]

5. Morgan adjusted the drone's altimeter control. Its video feed showed his creation zipping over a fountain, barely avoiding the spray that could short circuit its damaged electronics. He <u>cleared his throat</u>. *Whew, that was close!*

The drone dipped into an alley and careened around a corner. Out onto Monderson Avenue. Over pedestrians and sidewalk vendors.

Without warning, an open umbrella covered the camera lens and obliterated Morgan's view. He cursed. *Sabotage. Jacob.* It had to be Jacob. [Is this some kind of race with a prize for the winner? Is Morgan trying to deliver something of importance? Does his drone contain valuables he has robbed from Jacob? Maybe Jacob is an officer of the law.]

What's the big deal?

Charles Dickens, in the persona of Mr. Bumble, said that crying "opens the lungs, washes the countenance, exercises the eyes, and softens down the temper." Emotion should play a significant role in prose and poetry. Crying provides an excellent opportunity for that.

However, *cried* can turn into a repetition that makes readers *cry* because they're tired of seeing it.

Instead of making your characters cry, *show* their emotions.

A character might shed tears for many reasons:

Anguish, anxiety, defeat, denial, depression, desperation, embarrassment, guilt, humiliation, irritation, loneliness, pain, panic, pride (in someone else), rage, regret, relief, sadness, shame, sympathy

Here are just a few of the ways you could show these emotions:

Anguish
Sweating
Trembling
Cords standing out on neck
Clenching jaw or grinding teeth

Anxiety
Fidgeting
Wringing the hands
Rapid, shallow breathing
Clenching interwoven fingers

Defeat
Lack of eye contact
Slumped posture
Toneless dialogue
Trembling chin

Denial
Elevated eyebrows
Raised voice
Rapid speech
Wide eyes

Depression
Head in hands
Hunched shoulders
Shuffling feet, hands in pockets
Lowered head, with gaze on ground or toes

Desperation
Biting bottom lip
Darting gaze
Pacing
Tugging at hair

Embarrassment
Coughing
Excessive swallowing
Tugging at clothing
Wincing

Guilt
Cracking voice
Grimacing
Lip biting
Quivering chin

Humiliation
Blushing
Bowing the head
Hiding the face
Hugging oneself

Irritation
Cursing
Stomping
Snorting or sneering
Ill-considered dialogue

Loneliness
Monotone voice
Talking to oneself
Watching sad movies or TV series
Excessive time on internet or playing video games

Pain
Flinching
Grimacing
Clutching the painful area
Writhing or bending over

Panic
Incoherence
Rasping breaths
Squeezing eyes shut
Flinching at unexpected sounds

Pride (in someone else)
Elevated chin
Gleam in the eyes
Pointing at the object of one's pride
Discussing the accomplishment with someone nearby

Rage
Crossed-arm stance
Flared nostrils
Puckered forehead
Physical or verbal attacks

Regret
Downturned lips
Frail voice
Attempting to explain or apologize
Trying to right the wrong that caused the regret

Relief
Hesitant laughter
Huge exhalation
Relaxing posture, especially shoulders
Gazing up, pressing palms together in a praying gesture

<u>Sadness</u>
Puffy face or eyes
Runny makeup
Snot on upper lip or mustache
Swiping at nose with tissue

<u>Shame</u>
Flushed cheeks
Moaning
Vibrating chin
Poor personal grooming

<u>Sympathy</u>
At a loss for words
Sad smile
Verbal offer of assistance
Murmuring optimistic platitudes in a soothing tone

If you have room, try *showing* instead of *telling*.

With the suggestions in the previous section, we can eliminate *cried* in a few examples. Feel free to snag them as story prompts.

Jenna <u>cried</u> loudly.

Why?

Jenna's chin vibrated. "I'm so sorry," she said with a loud moan.

Having Jenna cry loudly tells us something but provides no visuals. The second sentence gives an immediate mental image and lets us know, with both her words and her body language, that she's crying to express shame.

When I telephoned David, he <u>cried</u>.

Why? This scenario leaves no room for David's body language if we want to maintain strict point of view. The narrator can't see his reaction. However, the writer can relay any sounds he makes.

When I telephoned David, I heard nothing on the other end of the buzzing line. For a moment, I thought he had hung up on me. Then hesitant laughter rumbled above the static. "Thank God you're safe," he said.

Same situation. Added details and drama. Readers will know David is relieved.

Justin cried during the medal awards ceremony.

Was Justin crying tears of relief? Was he sad because he didn't receive an award?

Justin's six-year-old daughter marched onto the stage to receive her medal of bravery. He leaned toward the stranger sitting on his left. "Y'know, she just about lost her own life rescuing that little boy."

With a few more details, we learn how Justin's daughter earned her medal and that he's proud of her.

The baby cried at the drop of a hat.

This sentence provides no reason for the crying, and *at the drop of a hat* is cliché. Can we provide a reason for the baby's crying? Panic, perhaps, or pain?

Several times hourly, the baby screamed and beat at its tummy with its tiny fists.

Pain is the motivation.

What about panic?

Every time the phone rang or a door slammed, the baby flinched and wailed.

I took *wailed* from the word list that follows and combined it with body language to provide a more vivid description.

Animals cry too.

We can compare cries to sounds such as *yowling* and *mewling*. These types of words work particularly well when the sounds match the descriptions of our characters.

A professor who has large, owl-like eyes might *hoot* when she cries.

A donkey-faced construction worker might *bray*.

Bullies who pursue their prey like a pack of dogs might *yelp* when their victim turns on them to defend himself.

Because real men don't cry?

The following sentences assume feminine gender for their protagonists. Change at will to suit your characters, remembering that some of these are cliché.

- A storm of tears raged in her eyes.

- Her cheeks shone with moist pride and regret.

- Her eyes gushed.

- Her eyes misted.

- Her eyes moistened.

- Her eyes welled with tears.

- Her lashes grew heavy with tears.

- Her pain released in a torrent of tears.

- Salty tears tunneled their way into her mouth.

- She blinked briny tears.

- She choked up.

- She turned on the waterworks.

- She wiped her eyes.

- Sorrow rained from her eyes.

- The dam of sorrow burst, releasing a flood of tears.

- The faucet of grief opened, gushing salty tears onto her cheeks.

Exercises and story prompts.

Try to eliminate *cried* from each of the following examples.

1. Sushi <u>cried</u> and barked in the kitchen. Bob rolled over in bed to peer at the clock: 3:07 a.m.

"Three times in less than an hour," he muttered as he threw on his robe and lumbered out of the bedroom. "For cryin' out loud, what's got into you, dog?"

A thunderous pounding on the back door vibrated the windows.

The hairs on the back of Bob's neck bristled.

2. Tammy <u>cried</u> and pushed Ansel away. "You don't understand," she said. "I want out. Now."

He grabbed a pillow off the bed. "You want *out*?"

She staggered backward, her retreat thwarted by the wall.

Ansel stalked toward her, pillow clutched in his hammy fists.

3. Heath Stoltz <u>cried</u> as his granddaughter Emily glided down the aisle toward her groom, Gardner Wheaton. Why hadn't Heath told her the truth about Gardner? Would she have agreed to marry him if she had known?

Verbs and phrases you could use to replace *cried*.

<u>A</u>
Agonized, anguished

<u>B</u>
Bawled, bayed, beat one's breast, bemoaned, bewailed, bleated, boo-hooed, blubbed, blubbered, broke down, burst into tears

<u>C</u>
Caterwauled

<u>D</u>
Despaired, dripped tears

E
Eyes welled with emotion

G
Grieved, grizzled, groaned

H
Hooted, howled

K
Keened

L
Lamented

M
Mewled, moaned, moped, mourned

N
Nose bubbled

P
Pined, puled

R
Rained teardrops

S
Screamed, shed tears, shrieked, shrilled, sniffled, sniveled, snuffled, sobbed, sorrowed, squalled, squealed

T
Turned on the tears

U
Ululated

W
Wailed, wauled, wawled, wept, whimpered, whined, whooped, wrawled

<u>Y</u>
Yauped, yawled, yawped, yelped, yipped, yowled

Frown or Scowl

Do your characters frown or scowl whenever they're angry or upset? These facial expressions are easy to think of while writing a first draft. However, sometimes they multiply, like fleas on a stray dog, until you find them hiding on almost every page.

Why do your characters frown or scowl?

Facial expressions are more than action tags. Every movement of the face should advance your story. A scowl or frown could be the result of:

Aggravation, aggression, agitation, anger, belligerence, concentration, confusion, constraint, contemplation, defeat, defiance, denial, determination, disagreement, disappointment, disapproval, disbelief, discomfort, doubt, embarrassment, exasperation, impatience, insecurity, introspection, irritation, nervousness, oppression, pessimism, shame, skepticism, stubbornness, uncertainty, unease, worry

Explore alternative body language.

Imagine your appearance when you're aggravated. Better yet, stand in front of a full-length mirror, act aggravated, and study your reflection. How are you standing? Where are your hands and fists? Is your head straight, cocked, or thrust forward? Study the color of your cheeks, the set of your jaw, and the movement of your nose. Now you can describe an aggravated protagonist without either the *F-* or *S-*word.

Try the above exercise whenever you see *frown* or *scowl* in your work. Decide what emotion your character is experiencing and substitute different body language.

Here are a few options to get you moving in the *write* direction:

Aggravation
Clenched jaw
Crossed arms
Pacing
Tapping foot

Aggression
Curled upper lip
Finger pointing
Flared nostrils
Leaning into someone else's personal space

Agitation
Pacing
Jerky movements
Restlessness
Wavering voice

Anger
Bared teeth
Flared nostrils
Stamping a foot
Wide-legged stance

Belligerence
Clenched fists
Fixed glare
Jutting jaw
Loud voice

Concentration
Fixed gaze
Dilated pupils
Fingers stroking chin
Minimal dialogue

Confusion
Stuttering
Biting the lip
Rubbing the chin
Exaggerated swallowing

Constraint
Bowed head
Minimal eye contact
Stepping or leaning back
Picking at lint or animal hairs on clothing

Contemplation
Relaxed posture
Studying ceiling or toes
Chewing on a pen or pencil
Leaning back in chair with arms behind head

Defeat
Vibrating chin
Sagging posture
Non-responsiveness
Staring at toes or hands

Defiance
Cocked head
Grinding teeth
Puffed-out chest
Stony stare

Denial
Slack jaw
Wide eyes
Backing away
Raising palms and shaking the head

Determination
Clenched fists
Jaw thrust forward
Pushing up sleeves
Steepled fingers

Disagreement
Crossed arms
Shaking head
Twitching nose
One leg crossed over the other in seated position

Disappointment
Hard swallow
Shuffling feet
Stolid expression
Wincing or flinching

Disapproval
Tight lips
Constricted pupils
Outstaring someone
Walking away without letting someone finish their sentence

Disbelief
Palm on chest
Rapid blinking
Turning pale
Unfocussed gaze

Discomfort
Shuffling feet
Pained grimace
Rubbing back of neck, chin, or forehead
Repeatedly shifting body weight from one foot to the other

Doubt
Biting the cheek
Rocking on the feet
Forcing the lips together
Cramming hands in pockets

Embarrassment
Blushing
Coughing
Sweating
Wincing or flinching

Exasperation
Making a rude gesture
Scoping out the ceiling
Running fingers through hair
Raising hands in an *I-give-up* gesture

Impatience
Crossing the arms
Watching the door
Repeatedly checking the time
Standing akimbo (hands on hips, elbows turned out)

Insecurity
Closed posture
Fiddling with hair or biting nails
Hiding hands in pockets or behind back
Checking one's breath behind an open hand

Introspection
Quiet mood
Lowered head
Glancing downward during conversation
Gazing past/around someone while speaking

Irritation
Arguing
Crossing the arms
Narrowing the eyes
Raising the voice

Nervousness
Dilated pupils
Drumming fingers
Excessive blinking
Rapid breathing

Oppression
Slow, soft speech
Teeth clamped on upper lip
Folded hands and bowed head
Standing with weight on one leg, other leg angled away from body

Pessimism
One hand on hip
Wide eyes
Lopsided sneer
Single arched eyebrow

Shame
Crying
Involuntary moan
Hiding the face with hair or hat
Scuffing a toe against carpet or dirt

Skepticism
Wrinkled nose
Hand gesture of dismissal
Condescending smile
Cutting someone off in mid-sentence

Stubbornness
White knuckles
Fixed stare
Set jaw
Tapping foot

Uncertainty
Shrugging
Rubbing the chin
Tugging on the lip
Interrupting one's own dialogue

Unease
Clammy hands
Picking at food
Licking or biting the lips
Repetitive actions that accomplish nothing

Worry
Poor sleep habits
Poor personal grooming
Puffy eyes with dark pouches beneath
Calling police or other support services

Google Images provides interesting alternatives.

Search images.google.com for emotions such as *angry* or *confused*. You'll find a multitude of graphics that show body language.

Ditto for *YouTube*.

Videos add sound and movement. An angry tycoon who trumpets like an elephant packs more of a punch than a frowning boss, don't you think?

Consider two excerpts.

Which of the following do you prefer?

First version:

Bruce <u>frowned</u> deeply when he saw the dark expression on Debbie's face.

She <u>scowled</u>. "Why do you always act like such an idiot whenever my parents come to visit?"

"Because I ..." He <u>frowned</u> once more. "Maybe because your mother makes me feel like a useless insect, and your father swears so much I want to beat the crap out of him."

Second version:

Bruce <u>recoiled</u>. Debbie's flared nostrils signaled warfare.

Her <u>face twisted</u>. "Why do you always act like such an idiot whenever my parents come to visit?"

"Because I ..." He crossed his arms and <u>bit his lip</u>. "Maybe because your mother makes me feel like a useless insect, and your father swears so much I want to beat the crap out of him."

Same dialogue, same number of words, but isn't the body language in the second version more effective at telling the story?

Do you need direct replacements? Check this list.

For those occasions when you require a quick *insert-here* approach for *frown* or *scowl*, try a word or phrase from the following list.

<u>B</u>
Beetle the brow, blanch, blench, boo, brood

C
Cloud up, clump brows together, contemplate, contort one's face, converge eyebrows, cower, crease the brow, cringe, crinkle the brow

D
Deliberate, do a slow burn

F
Furrow the brow

G
Give a dirty look, give a withering look, give the evil eye, give/make a moue, glare, gloom, glower, grimace, grovel

H
Hiss, hoot, huff, humph

I
Imitate Grumpy Cat

K
Knit brows together

L
Look angrily, look askance at, look black, look daggers, look stern, look sullen, lour/lower

M
Make a pained expression, make a wry face, menace with the eyes, mope, mull, muse

N
Narrow one's eyes

P
Ponder, pooh-pooh, pout, pucker the forehead, pull a face

Q
Quail

R
Recoil, reflect, ruck/ruckle the brow, ruminate

S
Scourge with a stare, screw up one's face, scrunch up the face, shrink, shy away, simper, size up, smirk, sneer, snicker, sniffle, snigger, snort, sob, sour one's smile, squinch, squint, stare angrily, stare icily, sulk

T
Turn away, twist the face, twitch

W
Wax glum, wax morose, weep, wrinkle the brow

Great or Awesome

People often say *great* and *awesome* in dialogue. The words are also common in children's or YA fiction. With that in mind, I created the following list. You'll note a large number of clichés, which are appropriate for the above types of writing if not overused.

However, before you get to the list, consider the alternatives.

Whenever you find yourself abusing hackneyed adjectives, try substituting body language. Scrutinize the following paragraph pairs and decide which of each provides the best effect.

Eve's new tattoo was <u>great</u>.

Adam's eyes bulged when Eve flashed her new tattoo. He staggered back a step.

You must set the stage for this type of interaction. Adam's body language could just as easily indicate disapproval.

Adam's chest was <u>awesome</u>.

Adam's chest flexed, tiny pearls of perspiration reflecting the dim light. Eve gasped.

Readers should have no doubt about the reason for Eve's gasp in this example.

"You're a really <u>awesome</u> girl," Adam said to Eve.

Adam pulled Eve closer and kissed her in a way that left no doubt about his feelings for her.

Once again, further context isn't required. With a combination of body language *(show)* and narrator's observation *(tell)*, readers have a clear picture of Adam's feelings.

Eve ate the <u>awesome</u> spaghetti.

Eve devoured the spaghetti and licked the plate clean.

More context would show whether Eve devours the spaghetti because she's hungry, or because she enjoys the meal.

"Your grandfather is <u>great</u>," said Adam.

"I can't believe your grandfather bequeathed so much money to the Red Cross," said Adam.

For this to work, readers must know that Adam approves of the grandfather's actions. The second paragraph could just as easily be a negative comment if the old man donated to the Red Cross at the expense of his family.

In each example, the second paragraph is longer. If economy of words is crucial, you might have to resort to more *tell* and less *show*.

Are you ready for the list?

Ways to say *great* or *awesome*:

<u>A</u>
A-1, ace, admirable, amazing, astonishing, astounding, awe-inspiring

<u>B</u>
Bad, bang-up, best, beyond the call, blue-chip, blue-ribbon, boss, breathtaking, brilliant

<u>C</u>
Capital, captivating, cat's meow, cat's pajamas, clever, colossal, commendable, cool, copacetic

<u>D</u>
Dandy, dazzling, delightful, diving

<u>E</u>
Engaging, enjoyable, epic, excellent, exceptional, exciting, exemplary, exquisite, extraordinary

<u>F</u>
Fabulous, fantabulous, fantastic, far-out, fine, finest, first-class, first-rate, flawless, fly, four-star, front-page

G
Glorious, gnarly, good, grand, great, groovy

H
Heart-stopping, heavenly, hip, huge, humbling, hunky dory

I
Illustrious, impressive, incomparable, incredible, ingenious, intense, invaluable

K
Kind

L
Laudable, lovely

M
Magnificent, majestic, major-league, marvelous, masterful, mind-blowing, mind-boggling, miraculous, momentous, monumental, moving

N
Neat, nifty, not too shabby, notable, noteworthy

O
Out of sight, out of this world, outstanding, overwhelming

P
Peachy, peerless, perfect, phantasmagorical, phenomenal, pleasant, polite, powerful, praiseworthy, premium, priceless, primo, prodigious

R
Rad, radical, refreshing, remarkable, righteous

S
Sensational, shazam, sick, singular, smashing, solid, special, spectacular, splendid, splendiferous, splendorous, staggering, standout, state-of-the-art, stellar, sterling, striking, stunning, stupendous, sublime, super, superb, super-duper, superior, superlative, supreme, surprising, sweet, swell

T
Terrific, the bee's knees, the bomb, thrilling, thumbs-up, tiptop, top-drawer, topflight, top-notch, top-of-the-line, transcendent, tremendous

U
Unbelievable, uncommon, unique, unmatched, unparalleled, unprecedented, unreal

W
Way-out, wicked, wild, wonderful, wondrous, world-class, wow

Z
Zero cool

Heart Pounded

Do you fall back on the *heart pounded* phrase whenever your characters are afraid or stressed? Guess what, dear writer. There's a cure for that.

Ask yourself *why?*

Before considering alternatives, you need to know *why* your protagonist's heart is pounding.

Here are just a few activities, emotions, and external factors that could make a person's heart beat faster:

- Physical exertion like climbing, running a marathon, or swimming several lengths of the pool.

- Dehydration.

- Stress or conflict.

- Phobias and fears, which might also escalate into a panic attack.

- Sexual desire, love.

- Annoyance with telemarketers, noisy dogs, door-to-door salespeople, slow restaurant service.

- Anticipation before attempting something like public speaking or cliff jumping.

- Other strong emotions such as anger, anxiety, defeat, disappointment, enthusiasm, excitement, fear, nervousness, worry.

- Mitral valve disease, tachycardia, or heart attack.

- Many other medical conditions.

- Hormonal changes.

- Caffeine, nicotine, alcohol.

- Medications such as decongestants, diet pills, asthma inhalers.

- Some herbal preparations.

- Street drugs such as amphetamines and cocaine.

Consider other possibilities.

Once you've determined the reason for the pounding heart, investigate different ways of peeking behind the curtain. Although some of the following might be deemed cliché, evaluate physical manifestations you could substitute instead:

- Racing pulse.

- Rising temperature.

- Light-headedness.

- Tingling skin.

- Breathlessness.

- Wheezing.

- An unpleasant taste in the mouth.

- Dry mouth or tongue.

- Hyperventilation.

- Dizziness.

- Flushing face, neck, and upper torso.

- Shivering.

Dialogue can treat the *heart pounded* disease while maintaining point of view.

Unless you're an omniscient narrator, you can't know what other people in your piece are feeling.

You might notice Jordan's wheezing or flushing, but you would be unable to perceive an unpleasant taste in his mouth or his racing pulse. When Jordan experiences these physical signs, he might make a sour face and announce:

"That tastes horrible. Did you put MSG in it? My pulse is racing like a freight train."

Yes, Joe used a cliché, but it's all right. He's speaking in character.

Cowboy Ken, our POV character, might declare his love for Susan something like this:

"Gosh darn it, Susie, can't you tell how I feel about you? I'm all lathered up like an old stud horse chasin' after a filly, and my heart's poundin' like a blacksmith's hammer in my chest. C'mon, give me a chance. Please?"

Susan has a pounding heart too, but maybe you can introduce a hurdle:

Susan gazed at Ken from behind her fan. "You know I could never love you. You don't have two cents to rub together in the pockets of those threadbare jeans, and I'm already promised to another."

Her red cheeks and bright eyes reminded Ken of a mare in heat. Shucks. She was lying.

It's up to readers to decide whether Ken has interpreted her feelings correctly. Of course you *will* provide clues or misdirection as appropriate, won't you?

Now we get to the list of direct replacements for *pounded*.

Note that some of these verbs are *tells*, which are appropriate when word count is limited. For instance, a groaning heart paints a different picture than a cartwheeling one. In each case, a single word tells how the protagonist is feeling.

A jackhammering heart could be the result of many emotions, which you can show elsewhere in your story or poem. Likewise with a rocketing or galloping heart. Consider the subtle nuances of each verb before choosing it.

A
Ached

B
Banged, beat, bounced, bounded, bumped

C
Capered, careened, careered, cartwheeled, cavorted, convulsed

D
Danced, drummed

E
Exploded

F
Faltered, fell, flailed, flapped, flip-flopped, flounced, fluttered, frolicked, froze

G
Galloped, galumphed, gamboled, groaned

H
Hammered, heaved, hopped, hurdled

I
Jackhammered, jerked, jigged, jogged, joggled, jounced, juddered, jumped

K
Knocked

L
Leaped/leapt, lurched

P
Palpitated, pitched, plummeted, pranced, pulsated, pulsed, pumped

Q
Quaked, quavered, quivered

<u>R</u>
Raced, raged, reeled, reveled, rocketed, rollicked, romped

<u>S</u>
Shuddered, sighed, skipped, soared, somersaulted, sped, sprinted, stormed, strutted, swaggered

<u>T</u>
Thrashed, throbbed, thudded, thumped, tossed, trembled, trotted, tumbled, turned to lead, twitched

<u>V</u>
Vaulted, vibrated

<u>W</u>
Writhed

Laughed or Smiled

Do you depend on *smiled* or *laughed* too often in your writing? This chapter provides alternatives. Before studying the list, though, consider the other possibilities available to you.

Rather than rely on direct phrases such as *she snickered*, try body language, weather, and surroundings to *show* the happiness of your characters:

His eyes crinkled at the corners.

The glowing appreciation on her face shone brighter than the noonday sun.

She hummed softly, a sparkle in her eyes.

Her voice grew bubbly.

He slapped the table and doubled over with mirth.

Add laughter with dialogue.

"Ha ha."

"Tee hee."

"Mwah ha ha."

"Heh heh."

"That's funny."

"You're a hoot."

"I tell ya, Harry, that there gal looks like she done swallowed the entire Cheshire Cat."

Clichés have their place. Be careful, though. Not all pieces lend themselves to this type of writing:

He brought the house down.

She sent everyone into convulsions.

The audience rolled in the aisles.

The comedian's barrel-of-laughs routine earned him a recurring gig at The Comedy Club.

Rather than repeat the familiar and often mundane, invent a phrase. Idioms weren't considered trite the first time they were written. In each case, someone produced an imaginative phrase that appealed to the public. Over time, it joined the ranks of clichés shunned by authors and poets.

Who knows? Your turn of phrase could become as popular as *He laughed all the way to the bank.*

Try sentences like these:

His shoulders shook so hard he peed himself.

Wilma spewed coffee down the front of Fred's shirt. Hmm, he thought, I didn't realize the joke was so funny.

Harry didn't respond but held his sides as though he had a stomachache. I studied his face. The subtle upward quirk of his mouth told me he was smothering a laugh.

If your word count isn't restricted, try making a person's laugh a character trait in longer passages such as the following:

A smirk replaced his frown of suspicion, and then the room resounded with his distinctive laugh, akin to the heavy bellowing of a donkey before it reaches full bray. He pushed his chair back and met me halfway across the office, where we thumped each other on the back.

The noise Penny made came from deep within her throat, reminiscent of a snorting pig—apropos for her snout nose and pink complexion.

Avoid acronyms such as *LOL* and *ROFL* unless you're writing a piece that incorporates text messages.

You can't wax poetic with every sentence you write. Too much fluff and you bore readers, or an editor might brand your writing with the dreaded *purple prose* label.

Adjectives to describe smiles.

A
Abrupt, affectionate, agreeable, airy, ambrosial, amiable, amused, angelic, angry, answering, antiseptic, apologetic, approving, ardent, artificial

B
Backward, bashful, beaming, beatific, beautiful, beguiling, benign, big, bitter, bland, boyish, brave, brilliant, brittle, broad, buoyant

C
Calm, cautious, charming, cheerful, cheesy, childlike, clear, complacent, conceited, conciliatory, condescending, conscious, contagious, contemptuous, convenient, counterfeit, courageous, courteous, covert, crafty, crooked, curdled, curious, cynical

D
Dazzling, deadly, debonair, delightful, deprecating, derisive, devilish, diabolical, dim, disarming, disdainful, doubtful, dubious

E
Eager, enamored, endearing, endless, engaging, enormous, envious, excited, exultant

F
Facile, faded, faint, fake, false, fascinated, fawning, fitful, flattering, fleeting, forced, frank, frigid

G
Gentle, ghastly, girlish, glib, glowing, gracious, grave, greasy, grim, gummy

H
Haughty, hideous, hollow, hospitable, humorless, hungry

I
Icy, idiotic, immutable, impish, imploring, inane, incandescent, incisive, incredulous, indifferent, indomitable, indulgent, infectious, ingratiating, innocent, insipid, inviting, involuntary, ironical, irrepressible

J
Joyless, joyous

K
Kind

L
Languid, lazy, listless, little, lovely, loving, lurid

M
Malevolent, malicious, maternal, meaning, meek, melancholy, mellow, metallic, mirthless, mischievous, mocking, Mona Lisa, morose, mournful, murderous

N
Naked, nasty, natural, naughty, nervous

O
Obnoxious

P
Parting, passing, paternal, patient, patronizing, peculiar, peerless, pensive, pert, phony, pitying, placid, playful, polished, polite, practiced, provocative

Q
Quiet, quizzical

R
Radiant, rapid, rare, rascally, ravishing, ready, reassuring, regretful, religious, reluctant, responding, restless, restrained, ridiculous, roguish, rueful, rustic

S
Sad, sagacious, sarcastic, sardonic, satirical, saturnine, saucy, scornful, seductive, serene, severe, sexy, shadowy, shy, sickly, sidelong, simulated, sinister, slow, sly, smarmy, somber, sparkling, speculative, spicy, sudden, sunny, superior, surprised, sustained, sweet, sympathetic

T
Thin, timid, timorous, tolerant, tortured, tremulous

U
Uncontrolled, unconvincing, unctuous, uneasy

V
Vague, vapid, vivacious

W
Wan, wanton, warm, watery, weary, welcoming, whimsical, wide, wild, winning, wistful, withering, wondering, wry

Adjectives to describe laughter.

A
Acerbic, airy, appreciative

B
Bitter, boisterous, booming, boyish, brassy, braying, breathless

C
Cacophonous, caustic, childish, coarse, contemptuous, controlled, convulsive, cordial, critical, cruel, curt

D
Deep, delighted, demonic, derisive, derogatory, discordant, disdainful, disparaging, dissonant, distant, drunken

E
Ear-splitting, earthy, easy, exasperated, excited, exquisite

F
Feminine, feverish, fiendish, foolish, forced, full-throated

G
Gentle, genuine, giddy, girlish, good-natured, grating, gruff, guilty, guttural

H
Harsh, hearty, helpless, hideous, high-pitched, hoarse, hollow, honest, husky, hysterical

I
Impulsive, inappropriate, incredulous, indulgent, inextinguishable, infectious, insolent, irrepressible, irreverent

J
Jeering, jittery, joyless

L
Light, lilting, liquid, loud, lusty

M
Malicious, malignant, maniacal, masculine, merry, metallic, mirthless, mocking, muffled, musical

N
Nervous, noisy

P
Piercing, polite

Q
Quiet

R
Ragged, rasping, raucous, resentful, restrained, ribald, rich, riotous, rowdy, rude

S
Sarcastic, sardonic, savage, scornful, self-deprecating, shaky, short, shrill, silent, silvery, smothered, soft, soulful, sour, spine-chilling, spontaneous, stifled, strident, sudden, suppressed, sweet

<u>T</u>
Teasing, throaty, triumphant

<u>U</u>
Uncontrollable, unnatural, unrestrained, uproarious

<u>W</u>
Wholesome, whooping, wild, wooden

Verbs and phrases to replace *laughed* or *smiled*.

If you've exhausted the alternatives, or economy of words is crucial, the following list could save you multiple trips to your thesaurus.

<u>A</u>
Arched one's lips

<u>B</u>
Babbled, bared one's gums, barked, bayed, beamed, bellowed, belly laughed, bent in two, bent over, boomed, brayed, broke up, bubbled, burbled, bust a gut, bust up

<u>C</u>
Cachinnated, cackled, cawed, cheeped, chirped, chirred, chirruped, chittered, chortled, chuckled, clucked, convulsed, cooed, cracked a smile, cracked up, crooned, crowed, curled up the lips

<u>D</u>
Dimpled, doubled up

<u>F</u>
Flashed one's teeth, fleered, forced a smile, fractured

<u>G</u>
Giggled, grinned, guffawed, gurgled

<u>H</u>
Hee-hawed, honked, hooted, horse-laughed, howled

<u>J</u>
Jeered, jested, jiggled, joggled, joked, joshed, juddered

L
Leered, lost control, lost it

M
Made merry

N
Neighed, nickered

P
Peeped, purred

Q
Quacked, quaked, quavered, quirked up one's lips, quivered

R
Roared, rolled in the aisles, rolled on the floor, rumbled

S
Screeched, shook, showed one's teeth, shrieked, simpered, smiled, smirked, snickered, sniggered, snorted, snuffled, split one's sides, spluttered, squawked, squeaked, squealed

T
Teased, tee-heed, thundered, tittered, trilled, trumpeted, tweeted, twinkled, twittered

V
Vibrated

W
Warbled, whickered, whinnied, whooped, wrinkled into a grin

Y
Yelped, yowled

Little

We've all heard the adage that *little* things can make a *big difference*. Unfortunately, too many *little* repetitions can make a *big difference* in writing too, maybe even enough to scare away readers.

One word, multiple shades of meaning.

Little can refer to size: a *little* fish.

It might mean a small amount: a *little* soya sauce.

People say it to stress a point: "There's *little* chance of that happening."

Little could signify a small degree: *little*-understood facts.

It can emphasize the smallness of an amount: a *little* bit.

Because the word has so many nuances, it creeps into writing unawares.

Let's edit *little* out of a few example sentences.

The changes are simple. I won't comment on *show* vs. *tell* or other literary taboos.

Add a little baking soda to your coffee to lower its acidity.

Add a pinch of baking soda to your coffee to lower its acidity.

A pinch provides an exact amount. Readers with GERD might even try this. (It works, by the way.)

He's too little to go on the roller coaster.

He's too short to go on the roller coaster.

You've probably seen the signs YOU MUST BE THIS TALL posted outside many amusement rides. Height should be expressed as *short* or *tall*, not *little* or *big*.

I think I'm a <u>little</u> ineb … inebri … drunk.

I think I'm a <u>tad</u> ineb … inebri … drunk.

Hmm. Maybe a drunk person would use *little* instead of *tad*. We should keep our dialogue realistic, right?

She relaxed <u>a little</u> when she saw the clouds clearing.

She relaxed <u>slightly</u> when she saw the clouds clearing.

Did she relax just a bit? Or did she relax. Period. Maybe the qualifier is unnecessary.

The <u>little</u> dog ate like a horse.

The <u>runty</u> dog ate like a horse.

The second sentence provides a mental image of a tiny dog with a humongous appetite.

Let's look at a longer example.

Mr. Eldridge scowled. "I'm a <u>little</u> disappointed by your performance review, Girard." A <u>little</u> tic played at one corner of his mouth, and his beady <u>little</u> eyes darted back and forth as he shuffled through the pages of Girard's evaluation. "You have two choices. Take a <u>little</u> cut in pay or quit."

Girard made a <u>little</u> choking sound in his throat. "A c-c-cut in pay? I c-c-can't afford that. My <u>little</u> girl needs special care, with her autism and all, and my wife just lost her job."

"Lost her job? That's why you've been a <u>little</u> distracted lately. I remember your wife. Well-qualified. Tell the <u>little</u> woman to contact Jolene in Human Resources. They need a new placement officer."

"Thank you sir, I—"

"You're welcome. Wifey can help you find a new job."

Most first drafts are rough. This one is no exception, with eight repetitions of *little*. Time to roll up the sleeves and make a few edits.

Mr. Eldridge scowled. *"I'm not happy about your performance review, Girard."* A tiny tic played at one corner of his mouth, and his ferret eyes darted back and forth as he shuffled through the pages of Girard's evaluation. *"You have two choices. Take a modest cut in pay or quit."*

Girard made a gurgling sound in his throat. "A c-c-cut in pay? I c-c-can't afford that. My first grader needs special care, with her autism and all, and my wife just lost her job."

"Lost her job? That's why you've been preoccupied lately. I remember your wife. Well-qualified. Tell the <u>little</u> woman to contact Jolene in Human Resources. They need a new placement officer."

"Thank you sir, I—"

"You're welcome. Wifey can help you find a new job."

The edited version retains one instance of *little*—plus *Wifey*—to show Mr. Eldridge's misogynistic attitude toward women. Changing the description of his eyes is classic *show*. The age of Girard's girl becomes tangible by describing her as a first-grader.

Do you hyphenate adjectives correctly?

As mentioned in other chapters, *The Chicago Manual of Style* recommends that writers hyphenate compound adjectives if they appear before nouns, but not after.

Compare the following examples:

*Tristan tossed a **peanut-sized** potato onto the compost pile.*

*The potato Tristan tossed onto the compost pile was **peanut sized**.*

*Wendi wore an **itsy-bitsy** bikini.*

*Wendi's bikini was **itsy bitsy**.*

Exercises and story prompts.

Edit the following, eliminating most instances of *little*. Feel free to use these as story prompts.

1. Nobody noticed the <u>little</u> insect scuttling across the floor. They were too busy clinking glasses, discussing their imaginary <u>little</u> problems, and laughing their fake <u>little</u> society laughs.

Josh smiled as he watched the wireless video feed broadcasting from his <u>little</u> bug, <u>*LittleEye Rov II*</u>. The rover drone followed Carmen and Vanessa into a bedroom and recorded their <u>little</u> tryst. It scrabbled into a closet and eavesdropped on the details of a <u>little</u> bribe between a contractor and the mayor.

Ahh, blackmail. A <u>little</u> here, a <u>little</u> there, a <u>little</u> more money in Josh's bank account. Life was good.

2. A solitary <u>little</u> star sparkled in the night sky. Wharton felt more than a <u>little</u> dazed. Where were the rest of the stars? He tried to remember.

His brain was a <u>little</u> fuzzy, but he recalled a <u>little</u> jolt. The cockpit of the <u>little</u> terrestrial exploration unit had flashed a brilliant laser blue, and everything had gone black.

Where was he? Where were the <u>little</u> rivulets of water, the vegetation, and the escarpments in the distance?

<u>Little</u> tremors shook the ground. He scrambled away from the rocks and sprawled face down in the sand, hands covering his head.

3. "A <u>little</u> more time. I just need a <u>little</u> more time." Erik sniffled. "I got a <u>little</u> money coming to me in two days. From Jenny. I'll pay. I promise I'll pay."

Rocco leaned against the doorjamb. "Yeah? That's what you said last week, you <u>little</u> loser. Your sis gonna give you enough to pay up?"

"Yes, I swear on my mama's grave and Jenny's life."

Jenny's voice sounded from somewhere behind Erik. "Rocco, you here again? Get out of here, you <u>little</u> bully."

Rocco backed away, <u>little</u> hands held high in surrender.

Jenny slammed the door in his face and stared down at her <u>little</u> brother. "Don't you go swearin' on Mama's grave or my life no more, you hear? Allowance day ain't 'til Friday, and you ain't givin' none of it to Rocco."

4. "Hey, Bobbie," Carlene called toward the den, "come to the bedroom quick if you want a <u>little</u> surprise."

Bare feet swished against the carpet in the hallway. Her husband's head appeared in the doorway. "A <u>little</u> surprise?" He tugged at his T-shirt. "I'm in—or at least I will be in a <u>little</u> minute."

"Not so fast, bucko. I think we've got our wires crossed."

Bobbie stopped, T-shirt half on half off, and scowled.

She held up her cell phone. "I just got a text from [Insert a character here. Bobbie's parents? Carlene's parents? An old girlfriend or boyfriend? Are they coming for a visit?]"

5. If Grayson held his breath just a <u>little</u> longer, he could make it. Just a <u>little</u> farther. So near. So—

His head broke the surface of the cove. A <u>little</u> runabout roared in his direction. He gasped and yelled, "Hey, over here."

The runabout continued its course straight toward him.

[What happens next? Does the runabout see Grayson? Does it collide with him? Why is he in the water? Suggestion: Look up the definition of *runabout*.]

6. A <u>little</u> knock sounded on the door. Greta laid aside the <u>little</u> booties she was knitting and plodded toward the foyer. She stood on her tiptoes to peer out the <u>little</u> peephole.

A wave of morning sickness swept over her. In a thin <u>little</u> voice, she mumbled through the door, "What do *you* want, loser?"

Gary answered, "[What does Gary say? Does it reveal something about his identity? He could be the baby's father, her brother, a drug dealer, her uncle, or a coworker. Why does she call him a loser? Can you reveal the details without making it seem like an infodump?]"

And now, the list.

You'll find alternatives that embrace the multiple meanings of *little*.

A
A bit of, a dab of, a dash of, a dribble of, a hint of, a modest amount of, a pinch of, a shade of, a small amount of, a smidgen of, a soupçon of, a speck of, a splash of, a spot of, a sprinkling of, a suggestion of, a suspicion of, a tad, a taste of, a touch of, a trace of, atom-sized, atomic, atrophied

B
Baby, bantam, bijou, bite-sized, bitty, brief, budding

C
Comminuted, compact, confined, confining, constrained, constricted, constringed, cozy, cramped, cubby

D
Dainty, de minimis, diminutive, dinky, dwarfed

E
Eensy, elfin, embryonic, exiguous

F
Faintly, fine, flea-sized, fledgling, fleeting, flyspeck, footling

G
Gnat-sized, gnomish

H
Half-pint, half-size, hardly any

I
Ickle, immature, indiscernible, infant, infinitesimal, insignificant, itsy-bitsy, itty-bitty

J
Junior, juvenile

K
Kitten-sized

L
Leprechaunesque, Lilliputian, limited, lowercase

M
Manikin, measly, micro-, micron-sized, microscopic, midget, mignon, mini-, miniature, minimal, miniscule, minor, minute, moderate, modest

N
Nanoscale, narrow, negligible, nit-sized, not much, not often

O
Olive-sized

P
Paltry, peanut-sized, peewee, petite, picayune, piddling, piffling, pigeonhole-sized, pilulous, pinprick-sized, pint-sized, pixie, pixie-like, pocketable, pocket-sized, poky, powdered, pulverized, puny, pygmy

R
Remotely, restricted, runty

S
Sawed-off, scant, scanty, scrimpy, short, short-lived, shrimpy, shriveled, shrunken, slight, slightly, small, small-scale, snug, some, somewhat, sparse, sprite-sized, sprouting, squat, stingy, stunted, subatomic

T
Tadpole-sized, teacup-sized, teensy, teeny-weeny, terse, thimble-sized, thumb-sized, tiddly, tiny, titchy, to a small extent, to some degree, toy, trifling

U
Underdeveloped, undersized

V
Vaguely, vertically-challenged, vest-pocket-sized

<u>W</u>
Wee, weensy, weeny

<u>Y</u>
Young

Look

Before you examine the following list, decide whether *look* is the word you need. Would something else be more appropriate for the situation? People can scowl, laugh, or hiccup. Even during romantic encounters, perhaps especially during romantic encounters, other body language might be more appropriate.

Can your protagonist point to something rather than *look* at it? Scowl at a salesman rather than *look* at him with an angry frown? Slurp steaming coffee and spit it all over herself rather than *look* at it and comment it's probably too hot to drink?

If you've considered the alternatives and decided a visual is required, step right up, flex your creative muscles, and proceed to the next paragraph.

You can swap *look* with many of the words in the list. Others need to be paired with *eyes, gaze,* or similar words.

For example, to use *dig into,* you could say "Jeremy's eyes dug into Jolene, his stare fixing her for so long she felt like a butterfly pinned to a mounting board." Some editors don't like eyes that perform independent actions, but this technique can add character to your work if not overdone.

Maintain point of view. You can say "Jeremy admired Jolene" as long as you're in Jeremy's head. If your story is from Jolene's point of view, you might have to convert the verb into an adjective and write something like "Jolene basked in Jeremy's admiring gaze."

The words in the list are seeds. For those seeds to flourish and become creative masterpieces, you must water with ingenuity and fertilize with imagination.

A
Admire, analyze, appraise, assess, audit

B
Beam, behold, blink, bore, browse

C

Canvass, compare, catch a glimpse of, catch sight of, check out, consider, contemplate, criticize, cross-examine

D

Dig into

E

Eagle-eye, evaluate, examine, exchange a glance, explore, eye, eyeball

F

Feast one's eyes, ferret, fix, flash, flirt with, focus on, follow, frisk over

G

Gander, gape, gawk, gawp, gaze, get a load of, give the once-over, glance, glare, glimmer, glimpse, gloat, glower, go through, goggle, grade, grill

H

Hunt

I

Inspect, interrogate, investigate

J

Judge

L

Lamp, lay eyes on, leaf through, leer, lift one's gaze, lock eyes, lower one's gaze

M

Make eyes, make out, measure, monitor, moon

N

Note

O

Observe, ogle, outstare, oversee

P

Pay attention to, peek, peer, peg, penetrate, perceive, peruse, pick over, pick through, pierce, pin, ponder, pore over, probe, pry, pump

Q

Question, quiz

R

Rake, read, reconnoiter, regard, review, riffle, rivet, rubberneck

S

Scan, scope, scout, scrutinize, search, see, share a look, shoot a glance, sift, sight, size up, skim, spot, spy, squint, stalk, stare, study, surveil, survey, sweep

T

Tackle, take a gander, take in, take notice, take stock of, throw a look, track, train eyes on

V

View, visualize

W

Watch, weigh, wink, winnow, witness

Z

Zero in

Look Like

An oft-overused construction in writing is *look like*. As with most phrases, it has its place.

Would the Douglas Adams passage from *Dirk Gently's Holistic Detective Agency* pack the same punch if we revised it? "If it looks like a duck, and quacks like a duck, we have at least to consider the possibility that we have a small aquatic bird of the family anatidae on our hands."

James Whitcomb Riley's original version is the one most people quote: "When I see a bird that walks like a duck and swims like a duck and quacks like a duck, I call that bird a duck."

Is anyone brave enough to do what Adams did with the duck adage and suggest an alternative for the following Oscar Wilde quote? "To lose one parent may be regarded as a misfortune; to lose both looks like carelessness."

A judicious sprinkle of *look like* throughout a novel works well. However, if you resort to this construction several times within the same chapter, readers will notice.

Sometimes you can remove the *look like* phrase without creating a direct replacement. Consider:

The large barbed-wire fence <u>looked like</u> a twisted tangle of tumbleweed.

The barbed-wire fence loomed large, a twisted tangle of confinement.

The second example presents a vivid image with a strong verb and a slight change from *tumbleweed* to *confinement*.

Consider the following sets of sentences. In each pair, the second example uses a word taken from the list at the end of this chapter.

Janie's eye creases made her <u>look like</u> an old elephant.

Janie's eye creases echoed those of an old elephant.

Do you see an old elephant's wrinkles? Maybe you envision an elephant mirrored in Janie's eyes.

In his crouched stance, he <u>looked like</u> a fierce panther.

His crouched stance exuded the ferocity of a panther.

A stealthy ferocity, fit for a panther's personality, is exemplified with *exuded. Oozed* would also fit.

With his tailored suit, he <u>looked like</u> a wealthy man.

His tailored suit trumpeted wealth and refinement.

Trumpet fanfare has announced the arrival of important dignitaries for centuries.

Are you convinced? Here's the list, an assortment of words and phrases that can function as verbs, adjectives, and nouns.

<u>A</u>
A chip off the old block, a mark of, accord with, adopt, affect, agree with, akin to, alike, allude to, analogous, announce, answer the description of, ape, appear, approach, approximate, assume the appearance of

<u>B</u>
Be redolent of, bear resemblance to, betray, border on, brim with, bring to mind, bristle with, broadcast

<u>C</u>
Call to mind, characterize, coincide with, come across as, come close to, come near, communicate, comparable with, conform to, connote, consistent with, convey, copy, correlate with, correspond to

<u>D</u>
Declare, denote, depict, designate, divulge, double, dovetail with, duplicate

E
Echo, emanate, embody, embrace, emit, emulate, epitomize, equal to, equate with, equivalent with, evocative of, evoke, exemplify, expose, exude

F
Fake, favor, feature, feign, fit

G
Give the impression of, have earmarks of

H
Have signs of, have the hallmarks of, herald, hint at

I
Identical to, illustrate, imitate, impersonate, imply, in harmony with, in the same league as, incarnate, indicate, indistinguishable, infer, insinuate, interchangeable, intimate

L
Limn

M
Manifest, match, mean, mention, mime, mimic, mirror, mock, model

N
Not unlike, notify

O
Offer, on par with, ooze

P
Paint, parallel, parody, parrot, pass for, personify, picture, point to, portend, portray, pose, possess, presage, pretend, proclaim, promise, propose

R
Radiate, redolent of, refer, reflect, reiterate, relate, relay, release, remind one of, reminiscent of, replicate, represent, resemble, resonate, reveal, reverberate

<u>S</u>
Same as, shout, show, signal, signify, similar to, simulate, smack of, sound like, spoof, square with, steer, strike one as, suggest, suggestive of, suit, symbolize, synonymous

<u>T</u>
Take after, tally with, teem with, tell, tend, the image of, the picture of, tout, transmit, trumpet, two of a kind, two peas in a pod, typify

<u>U</u>
Uniform

<u>V</u>
Verge on

<u>W</u>
Wear the mask of, wear the trappings of

Nauseated

Which word is correct: *nauseous* or *nauseated*?

Before considering other ways to say *nauseated* or *nauseous*, it's important to realize that many editors will tsk-tsk if they read something like *Bob felt nauseous*, preferring *Bob felt nauseated*.

Why?

Let's review an explanation from Vocabulary.com:

"If you're *nauseated,* you're about to throw up, if you're *nauseous,* you're a toxic funk and you're going to make someone else puke. These words are used interchangeably so often that it makes word nerds feel *nauseated.*"

Keep your editor happy, and choose *nauseated* for characters with queasy stomachs.

Capitalize on idioms.

Insides can turn to water. Characters' hearts can leap into their throats or mouths. Bowels can transform into jelly. Stomachs can sour.

However, rather than rely on idioms directly, analyze the meanings behind them to produce something more graphic.

Butterflies in the stomach

Butterflies? Ha! I had a whole swarm of bees in there.

Stomach doing flip flops or turning somersaults

John's stomach went into an instant rehearsal for the next Olympic Games gymnastics.

Stomach in a flap

A bevy of birds and bats flailed their wings in Sherry's stomach, bouncing between ribs and spine in a swelling frenzy of excitement.

<u>Stomach churns/lurches/tightens</u>

His bacon-and-eggs breakfast roiled in his belly.

Her stomach agitated and grumbled like an off-balance washing machine.

A sudden tautness assailed his middle, reminiscent of the tightrope he'd trod just moments before.

Create a memorable phrase.

My stomach is carousing with my kidneys.

His gut was knotted tighter than a hangman's noose round the neck of a 500-pound sumo wrestler.

Her insides smoldered like a nest of hatching dragon eggs.

Punch up your dialogue.

"I'm suffering from collywobbles."

"I've got an extreme case of the dithers."

Speaking of dialogue, let's keep it real.

Check this list of idioms for *to vomit*. In dialogue, anything goes. Your characters should sound like real people, not cardboard cutouts with perfect grammar.

<u>B</u>
Barf, bark at the ants, blow chunks, blow groceries, bob, boke it, boot, boot and rally, bow down before the porcelain throne, burl

<u>C</u>
Cack, call Ralph on the porcelain phone, call the whales, chuck, chuck one's cookies, chunder, cry Ruth

<u>D</u>
De-food, dial the porcelain phone, do the technicolor yawn, drive the porcelain bus, dry heave

86

E
Earl

F
Fail a fortitude save, feed the fish, fergle

G
Gack, gag, gragg

H
Heave, honk, horf, hork, hug the porcelain throne, hug the toilet, hurl

K
Kak, kiss Ralph

L
Laugh at the ground, laugh at the toilet, launch one's lunch, liquid laugh, lose one's lunch

M
Multicolor yawn

P
Paint the walls, park the tiger, pash the porcelain princess, pray to the great ceramic idol, pray to the porcelain god/goddess, psychedelic yawn, puke

R
Ralph, readjust fluids, retch

S
See one's lunch again, spew, suffer from motion sickness

T
Tactical chunder, talk to Ralph on the big white telephone, technicolor yawn, throw up, toss a sidewalk pizza, toss/woof one's cookies

U
Un-eat, un-swallow, upchuck, url, urp

<u>W</u>
Whistle beef, worship the porcelain throne, worship the ivory idol

Y
Yack, yarf, yark, yawn in technicolor, yodel groceries, york, yurp

Make the most of unpleasant nouns.

You could compare queasiness or nausea to a number of unpleasant things. Here are several to get you started.

(I had way too much fun with this part of the chapter.)

<u>B</u>
Baboon's butt, bad news

<u>C</u>
Camel spit, cat puke, cow slobber, crawling maggots

<u>D</u>
Decomposing meat, dirty ashtray, dirty diapers, dog's breakfast, dog vomit

<u>E</u>
Elephant ringworms, ex's cooking, ex's grumbling

<u>F</u>
Festering swamp, fried frog legs, frog in a blender, funeral, fur ball

<u>G</u>
Garbage, gargantuan booger

<u>H</u>
Hippo diarrhea, hyena crap

<u>K</u>
Kitty-litter box

<u>M</u>
Manure, mashed-up bugs, moldy mustard, moldy warts, monkey mucus

<u>O</u>
Offal, oozing bedsore, out-of-tune violin

<u>P</u>
Pig slop, plumber's butt, porta-potty, puréed grasshoppers

<u>R</u>
Rancid cheese, rat feces, road kill, rotten tomato, rotting haggis

<u>S</u>
Sewer, sinking boat, slimy cesspit, slithering slugs, snail slime, snake snot, squashed squid, steaming cow pie

<u>T</u>
Tainted hummus, teaming anthill, throbbing zit, toenail fungus, toilet

<u>W</u>
Weeping boil, wet cigarette butt, witch's cauldron, wormy liver

<u>Z</u>
Zombie brains

Exploit your imagination and experiences to generate fresh comparisons.

Invent new adjectives.

Add *able, al, est, esque, free, ful, ible, ic, ish, ive, less, like, oid, ous,* and other suffixes to nouns and verbs to create new adjectives.

Search for new words.

Explore a thesaurus for any of the words you find here. Judicious selection will show whether your protagonist is nervous, ill, or downright terrified.

But if you're on the search for speedy *nauseated* alternatives ...

... scour through this list of words and expressions. Some are colloquial and suitable for dialogue. Others are dated, apropos for period fiction.

A
Ailing, airsick, anemic, anxious, atremble

B
Barfy, bedridden, bilious, blah

C
Carsick, crummy

D
Debilitated, diseased, discombobulated, disoriented, distressed, dizzy, down, down in the mouth, drained, dreadful

E
Execrable

F
Failing, faint, febrile, feeble, feverish, foul, fragile, frail, fuddled

G
Giddy, green, green about the gills, groggy

H
Horrible, hurting

I
Icky, ill, in a bad way, in poor health, incapacitated, indisposed, infirm

L
Laid up, like death, lightheaded, lousy, low

M
Miserable, muzzy

N
Nasty, not so hot

O
Off, off-color, out of sorts

90

P
Peaked, poorly, pukey, puny, putrid

Q
Qualmish, queasy

R
Rocky, rotten, rough, run-down

S
Seasick, seedy, shaken, shaky, sick, sick as a dog, sick to the stomach, sickened, sickish, sickly, squeamish, stricken

T
Tormented, travel-sick, trembling, troubled

U
Uncomfortable, under par, under the weather, uneasy, unhealthy, unsettled, unsound, unstable, unsteady, unwell, upset

V
Vertiginous, vile

W
Weak, wobbly, woebegone, woozy, wretched

Y
Yucky

Nodded

Does this describe your writing?

- Your characters act like marionettes who nod ~~their heads~~ every few paragraphs, or worse, every few sentences. (Note the strikeout. What else would they nod? Their noses? Their knees?)

- You find yourself typing *nodded* to indicate approval or to sprinkle action beats throughout dialogue.

In your defense, perhaps you can't think of anything else.

What does a nod suggest?

To find a suitable substitution, you must know why your characters feel the need to nod.

Nodding can denote a plethora of emotions, including:

Acceptance or agreement, attentiveness or concentration, confidence, eagerness, excitement, greeting or recognition, satisfaction, smugness, support or sympathy, zeal

Head bobs and tosses signify disapproval in countries like Bulgaria, Turkey, and some parts of Greece and Italy. A nodding protagonist could make a story difficult to understand in these cultures.

Let's explore body language you could use instead.

Acceptance or agreement
Warm smiles
Leaning inward
Uncrossed arms
Unlocked ankles

Attentiveness or concentration
Wide eyes
Hint of a frown
Direct eye contact
Head forward or tilted

Confidence
Winking
Direct gaze
Wide stance
Firm handshake

Eagerness
Quick speech
Animated gestures
Fidgeting in one's chair
Finishing a task ahead of time

Excitement
Trembling
Hyperactivity
Loud speech
High-five or fist bump

Greeting or recognition
Hugging
Waving
Raising the eyebrows
Rushing toward someone

Satisfaction
Fist pump
Clap on the back
Puffed-out chest
Thumbs-up gesture

Smugness
Bragging
A smirk or sneer
Name-dropping
Swaggering or strutting

Support or sympathy
Hugging
Stroking someone's back
Fumbling for the right words
Squeezing someone's shoulder

Zeal
Flashing eyes
Frequent blinking
Rubbing hands together
Exaggerated movements

Removing *nodded* can strengthen your writing.

In your quest to eliminate *nodded*, you can add depth and emotion.

Consider the following unimaginative snippet.

Jennifer pulled her hair off her shoulders. "Can you please zip me up?"

Keith <u>nodded</u> as he reached for the zipper. "Sure."

"Ouch! Darn thing is too tight."

Keith <u>nodded</u>.

Besides being downright boring, the above passage repeats *nodded* twice. Let's amplify and add some tension.

Jennifer pulled her hair off her shoulders. "Can you please zip me up?"

Keith bit his lip as he reached for the zipper. "I can try."

"Are you saying I'm fat?"

His face turned a telltale shade of red.

With a bit of reorganization, the second passage employs a combination of *show* and *tell* to turn the encounter into something that could develop into humor or drama, depending on where the author decides to take it, without a single *nod*.

But when you need short and simple, try these replacements.

The following list provides precooked alternatives for *nodded*. They might bail you out if word count is limited or you want to intensify the pace of your piece.

A
Accepted, acknowledged, acquiesced, adopted, advocated, affirmed, agreed to, allowed, alluded, approved, assented, attested, authorized

B
Backed, bent the head, bent the knee, bobbed the head, bootlicked, bowed, brownnosed

C
Capitulated, ceded, certified, championed, cheered on, chose, complied, conceded, conceded defeat, concurred, confirmed, consented, corroborated, crawled, curtsied

D
Deferred to, dipped the head, dropped the head

E
Encouraged, endorsed, espoused

F
Facilitated, fancied, favored, fawned

G
Gave in, gave carte blanche to, gave one's blessing, genuflected, granted, green-lighted, groveled

H
Hinted

I
Implied, inclined the head, insisted

K
Kneeled, knelt, kowtowed

L
Let, lowered the head

O
Okayed, opted

P
Passed, permitted, preferred, proposed, prostrated

R
Ratified, recommended, relinquished, respected, responded affirmatively

S
Said yes, sanctioned, signaled, smiled, stooped, submitted, substantiated, succumbed, sucked, suggested, supported

T
Tilted the head, toadied, tolerated, truckled

U
Upheld, urged

V
Validated, verified, voted for, vouched for

W
Wagged the head, warranted, waved

Y
Yielded

Noisy or Loud

Are you tired of devising alternatives for *noisy* and *loud?*

Search no further.

Step closer, dear writer.

Closer.

Shush now while I invite you into the tranquility of my studio. Take a seat by the open wind—

What's that? A chainsaw? Perhaps a lawnmower? No, it has a high-pitched whirr. Aha! The neighbor is whipping weeds. Here. I have an extra set of earplugs for you. Put them in now before you get a headache. ...

Did I use *noisy* or *loud* in the previous paragraph? You already know what a chainsaw, lawnmower, and weed whipper sound like, so I'm guessing you heard the racket.

Merely incorporating loud objects in your poetry or prose can paint an effective picture. Or you can create comparisons.

His snoring, a dive bomber in my dreams, morphed into a sleepy wish for an extra pillow to smother the pilot.

The woodpecker's insistent rat-a-tat-tatting pounded like a jackhammer in my head.

***Loud* and *noisy* nouns could include:**

A
Airplane, air compressor, angry audience, angry banshee, avalanche

B
Backfiring auto, ballyhoo, bawling infant, bedlam, bomb, bragging wrestler, bulldozer

C
Cacophony, cascading waterfall, cattle stampede, chainsaw, chaos, clamor, cymbals

D
Dentist's drill, din, dive-bomber, drag race, drums

E
Earthquake, exploding [insert word]

F
Firecracker, fireworks, foghorn, food blender/processor, foofaraw, fracas, furor

G
Geyser, grenade, grinder, growling stomach, gunfire

H
Hailstorm, helicopter, hoo-haw, hoopla, hubbub, hullabaloo, hurricane

I
Ice grinder

J
Jackhammer, jet plane

L
Lawnmower, lovesick moose

M
Mayhem, motorboat, motorcycle, megaphone, meteor impact, murder (flock) of crows

N
Nagging spouse

O
Off-balance washer, off-key yodeler

P
Pack of bloodhounds, pandemonium, paper shredder, police siren, power washer, power sander

R
Racket, riot, rock concert, rock crusher, rock tumbler, rocket launch, roller coaster, ruckus, rumpus

S
Sandblaster, sander, screaming seagull, screaming skydiver, screeching parrot, siren, snowmobile, sporting event, sports bar, squealing brakes, stampede

T
Thunder, tornado, train collision, train whistle, trumpeting elephant, tuba, tumult

U
Uproar

V
Vacuum cleaner, volcano eruption

W
Whitewater rapids

Choose active verbs instead of adjectives.

Can you hear the sounds in the following sentences?

She stomped down the hall.

He thundered his displeasure.

The crowd roared its approval.

The train screeched to a stop.

Show the volume.

Her fierce retort pierced his eardrums.

The door slammed so hard it rattled the windows.

The wind screamed through every crevice it could find, freezing the fingers we held over our ears in an attempt to block its escalating volume.

Two cats yowled outside the house and woke the occupants from a deep sleep.

Stimulate the sensory palate.

Noisy and *loud* don't always refer to sound. The following sentence intertwines senses.

His tie with its riotous colors shrieked at me, begging to be ripped off and given a merciful death in the paper shredder.

Change adjectives into verbs to provide a different kind of multi-sensory approach.

The meadow's wildflowers trumpeted nature's tenacity, poking out through burnt roots and bushes within weeks of the forest fire.

Try these *loud* and *noisy* adjectives.

<u>A</u>
Amok

<u>B</u>
Banging, baying, bellowing, berserk, blaring, blasting, bleating, blustering, blusterous, blustery, boisterous, booming, brash, braying, buzzing

<u>C</u>
Cacophonous, caterwauling, chattering, clacking, clamant, clamoring, clamorous, clanging, clangorous, clanking, clattering, clattery, coarse, crashing

<u>D</u>
Deafening, dinning, discordant, dissonant, drumming

<u>E</u>
Ear-piercing, ear-popping, earsplitting, echoing

F
Fierce, forte, fortissimo

G
Grating, grinding, growling

H
Hammering, harsh, howling

I
Intense

J
Jangling, jarring

L
Loud, loudmouthed

O
Obstreperous, overloud

P
Penetrating, piercing, piping, plangent, pounding

R
Rackety, raging, rambunctious, ranting, rapping, rasping, raspy, raucous, resounding, reverberant, reverberating, ringing, riotous, rip-roaring, roaring, rolling, rowdy

S
Screeching, screaming, sharp, shrieking, shrill, squalling, stentorian, stertorous, strepitous, strident, stridulant, stridulous

T
Tempestuous, thumping, thundering, thunderous, trumpeting, turbulent

U
Unbridled, unrestrained, uproarious

<u>V</u>
Vocal, vociferant, vociferous, voluble

<u>W</u>
Wailing, wild

<u>Y</u>
Yelping

Said

He said. She said. They said.

Said is a convenient word when you need it, and some pundits claim you should never use anything else, *ever*, to attribute dialogue.

I disagree.

Please don't get huffy until you read the entire chapter, especially if you're a writer who swears on a bushel of Dothraki bells that *said* is the best way—nay, the only way—to tag conversation.

Repeat any word often enough, and it morphs into an irritation just as obnoxious as a saddle sore on a long ride.

Forget the rules. Invent your own. Whatever engages readers is right.

Consider the following micro-story.

An icy draft speared through the living room as John stepped into the house from the wintry blizzard that raged outside. His arms overflowed with packages.

"Please close the door," Amy <u>said</u>. "It's freezing in here."

John <u>said</u>, "Close it yourself!"

Amy <u>said</u> back, in an angry tone, "What did you say?"

"I told you to close it yourself," he <u>said</u>, in a voice so loud it rattled the windows.

She pressed her lips into a firm white line and <u>said</u>, "You're the one who pays the heating bill. But I guess you have lots of money. You can afford it."

He slammed the door ~~closed~~ and <u>said</u>, "If you'd get off your duff and find a job, I wouldn't have to pay all the bills myself."

Amy <u>said</u>, "Well, if you hadn't got me preg—"

"You're pregnant?" John <u>said</u>. "Why didn't you say something?"

Try this instead.

An icy draft speared through the living room as John stepped into the house from the wintry blizzard that raged outside. His arms overflowed with packages.

Amy glanced up from the baby booties she was knitting. "Please close the door. It's freezing in here."

John glowered. "Close it yourself!"

"What did you say?"

"I told you to close it yourself." The windows rattled. From the angry volume of his voice? Or the storm?

She pressed her lips into a firm white line. "You're the one who pays the heating bill. But I guess you have lots of money. You can afford it."

He slammed the door. "If you'd get off your duff and find a job, I wouldn't have to pay all the bills myself."

"Well, if you hadn't got me preg—"

"You're pregnant?" John beamed and dropped the packages. "Why didn't you say something?"

Did you notice the changes in the second piece?

1. Two paragraphs have no attribution. With an obvious back and forth of dialogue, it's unnecessary and distracting to tag every snippet of speech

2. Action beats replace dialogue tags in a few spots.

Amy glanced up ...
John glowered.
She pressed her lips ...
He slammed the door.
John beamed ...

3. The knitting of baby booties gives readers a clue about the ending, which comes as an abrupt surprise in the first piece.

4. One adjective, *angry*, describes John's attitude. Yes, it's a *tell*, and the pundits who recommend you should always *show* might disagree with its use. However, rules are made to be broken. Right?

5. One narrative statement becomes interrogative. Judicious use of questions can draw readers into prose or poetry.

Reread the pieces to see how much stronger the second example is. Both contain the same number of words.

Now consider a third version.

An icy draft speared through the living room as John stepped into the house from the wintry blizzard that raged outside. His arms overflowed with packages.

Amy glanced up from the baby booties she was knitting. "Please close the door. It's freezing in here."

John retorted, "Close it yourself!"

"What did you say?"

"I told you to close it yourself," he snapped. The windows rattled. Perhaps from the angry volume of his voice?

She pressed her lips into a firm white line. "You're the one who pays the heating bill. But I guess you have lots of money. You can afford it."

He slammed the door. "If you'd get off your duff and find a job, I wouldn't have to pay all the bills myself."

"Well, if you hadn't got me preg—"

"You're pregnant?" John beamed and dropped the packages. "Why didn't you say something?"

Did you catch the two *said* alternatives?

Retorted and *snapped* are so much more effective than *said*.

But don't overdo! Like exclamation points, em dashes, and ellipses, excessive use of colorful verbs for dialogue tags will irritate readers.

By the way, the third piece contains the same number of words as the first two.

And about that slamming door.

It's unnecessary to say someone slams a door *closed.*

Whenever you need a direct replacement for *said*, refer to this list.

Some of these words contravene the *show, don't tell* rule.

As always, watch for clichés and apply these suggestions sparingly. Some, while suitable for children, might not be appropriate for adults.

Words such as *neighed* or *whickered* can describe a character's voice, especially appropriate for someone with a horsey face. Frugal use recommended.

Although many writers show their characters laughing, sighing, sobbing, or breathing speech, I recommend you avoid verbs like these as dialogue tags. Save them for action beats, or substitute body language to show emotions.

If one of your characters *hisses* dialogue, at least one word in their speech should contain an *S*.

Lied or *doubted* and their ilk can break point of view if not used correctly. Many of these would be suitable for micro fiction where *tell* is often the norm, because *show* requires too many words.

A
Accepted, accused, acknowledged, acquiesced, added, addressed, adjured, admitted, admonished, advertised, advised, advocated, affirmed, agonized, agreed, alleged, announced, answered,

apologized, appealed, applauded, argued, arranged, articulated, asked, assented, asserted, asseverated, assumed, assured, attracted, averred, avowed

B

Babbled, badgered, barked, bawled, bayed, beamed, beckoned, began, begged, bellowed, bellyached, beseeched, bickered, blabbed, blathered, bleated, blubbered, blurted, boasted, boomed, bossed, bragged, brayed, breathed, bristled, broadcasted, broke in, bubbled, burbled, burped, burst out

C

Cajoled, called, carped, cautioned, censured, challenged, chanted, charged, chatted, chattered, cheered, chided, chimed, chimed in, chimed out, chirped, chittered, choked, chortled, chorused, chuckled, circulated, claimed, clamored, clarified, clucked, coached, coaxed, comforted, commanded, commented, complained, complimented, conceded, concluded, concurred, condemned, conferred, confessed, confided, confirmed, congratulated, consoled, contended, continued, contradicted, contributed, cooed, corrected, corroborated, counseled, countered, cried, cried out, criticized, croaked, crooned, crowed, cursed

D

Debated, decided, declaimed, declared, decreed, deduced, defended, demanded, demurred, denied, denoted, described, dictated, directed, disagreed, disclosed, disposed, disputed, disseminated, dissented, distributed, dithered, divulged, doubted, drawled, dribbled, droned

E

Echoed, effused, ejaculated, elucidated, emitted, empathized, encouraged, ended, entreated, exacted, exclaimed, explained, exploded, exposed, exulted

F

Faltered, fibbed, finished, fired back, framed, fretted, fudged, fumed, fussed

G

Gainsaid, gawped, gibbered, gibed, giggled, gloated, glowered, granted, greeted, grieved, grinned, griped, groaned, growled, grumbled, grunted, guaranteed, guessed, gurgled, gushed

H

Harangued, hectored, held, hesitated, hinted, hissed, hollered, howled, huffed, husked, hypothesized

I

Imitated, imparted, implied, implored, importuned, inclined, indicated, informed, inquired, insisted, instructed, interjected, interrupted, intoned, invited

J

Jabbered, japed, jeered, jested, jibed, joined in, joked, justified

K

Keened

L

Lamented, laughed, lectured, leered, lied, lilted, lisped

M

Made known, made public, maintained, marked, marveled, maundered, mentioned, mewled, mimicked, misquoted, moaned, mocked, mourned, mumbled, murmured, mused, muttered

N

Nagged, nattered, necessitated, neighed, nitpicked, noted

O

Objected, observed, obtruded, offered, opined, ordered

P

Panted, passed on, persisted, persuaded, pestered, piped, pleaded, pled, pledged, plowed on, pointed out, pondered, postulated, praised, prated, prattled, prayed, preached, premised, presented, pressed, presupposed, prevaricated, probed, proclaimed, prodded, professed, proffered, promised, promulgated, proposed, protested, provoked, publicized, published, puled, purred, put forth, put in, put out, puzzled

Q
Quaked, quavered, queried, questioned, quipped, quizzed, quoted

R
Raged, railed, ranted, rasped, rattled on, reasoned, reassured, rebuked, recalled, reckoned, recommended, recounted, reiterated, rejoiced, rejoined, related, released, remarked, remembered, reminded, remonstrated, repeated, replied, reported, reprimanded, reproached, reproved, requested, required, requisitioned, resounded, responded, resumed, retaliated, retorted, revealed, roared

S
Sang, sassed, scoffed, scolded, screamed, seethed, sent on, shared, shot, shouted, shrieked, shrilled, shrugged, shuddered, slurred, snapped, snarled, sniffled, sniveled, snorted, sobbed, solicited, sought, spat, specified, speculated, spluttered, spoke, spread, squeaked, squealed, stammered, started, stated, stormed, stressed, stuttered, suggested, supposed, surmised, swore

T
Tattled, taunted, teased, testified, theorized, threatened, threw back, thundered, ticked off, told, told off, touted, trailed off, transferred, transmitted, trembled, trilled, trumpeted, tutted

U
Understood, undertook, upbraided, urged, ushered forth, uttered

V
Verified, vociferated, voiced, volunteered, vouched, vowed

W
Wailed, wanted, warned, weighed in, went on, wept, wheedled, whickered, whimpered, whined, whinnied, whispered, whooped, wondered, worried

Y
Yakked, yammered, yawned, yawped, yelled, yelped, yowled

Sat

Sat **is devious.**

It sneaks into your writing while you're not looking.

It pretends to be innocent. Innocuous.

Until you read your story out loud, and the sibilant sounds of excessive *sat*s produce showers of spit that spray onto your screen.

Go ahead. Search your work in progress for *sat*, *sit*, *sits*, and *sitting*.

I'll wait.
...
......
....

How many did you find?

"The only thing that ever sat its way to success was a hen." ~ Sarah Brown

By finding imaginative verbs to replace most instances of *sit* in all its forms, you'll improve your writing.

Review the following sentences.

They <u>sat</u> in the booth.

Do you see people sitting in a restaurant booth?

They contorted themselves into the booth.

Now what do you envision? The booth might be smaller than usual, or the protagonists might have ample builds that make sitting difficult.

They collapsed into the booth.

Perhaps our protagonists haven't eaten for hours or days, and they're so hungry their legs won't hold them up any longer.

They luxuriated in the booth.

Do you picture patrons taking their time, perhaps sipping on several coffees while they enjoy the ambience?

They loitered in the booth.

This could be a setup for teenagers trying the patience of a server, while they occupy space that would be better utilized for a busy lunch crowd of customers who actually tip for good service.

It's all about motivation.

Consider a woman sitting on a seawall.

Does she *flop down on* the seawall while she relaxes after a long hike? Does she *balance on the edge* while she decides whether to jump into the deep water after a nasty breakup with her fiancé?

A carefully coined phrase will clarify a scenario when viewed in context.

Other ways to say *sat on* and *sat in*.

Some of the following phrases are colloquial. Select them only if appropriate. Better yet, invent something that might become the colloquialism of next year.

B
Balanced on the edge of
Basked in/on
Bestrode
Bowled oneself into/onto
Burrowed into/onto
Buried oneself in/on

C
Catnapped in/on
Chilled out in/on
Collapsed into/onto
Colonized
Cowered in/on
Cozied up to

Crumpled into/onto
Curled up in/on

D
Dawdled in/on
Dissolved into/onto
Dived/dove into/onto
Draped oneself over
Drooped into/onto
Dropped into/onto
Drove into/onto

E
Embedded oneself in/on
Ensconced oneself in/on
Enthroned oneself in/on
Entrenched oneself in/on

F
Fell into/onto
Flipped into/onto
Flopped down in/on
Flopped into/onto
Flung oneself into/onto
Futzed around in/on

G
Grafted oneself into/onto
Grabbed a seat/chair

H
Heaved oneself into/onto
Hung in/on
Hung over
Huddled in/on
Hunkered down in/on
Hurled oneself into/onto
Hurtled oneself into/onto

I

Idled in/on
Immersed oneself in/on
Implanted oneself in/on
Installed oneself in/on

K

Keeled over into/onto

L

Lay back in/on
Lazed in/on
Leaned back in/on
Lingered in/on
Loafed in/on
Lodged oneself in/on
Loitered in/on
Lolled in/on
Lollygagged in/on
Lounged in/on
Lowered oneself into/onto
Luxuriated in/on

M

Melted into/onto

N

Napped in/on
Nestled in/on
Nuzzled in/on

O

Occupied a seat/chair

P

Parked oneself in/on
Perched on the edge of
Pitched into/onto
Poised on the edge of
Positioned oneself in/on
Planted oneself in/on

Plonked down onto
Plopped down onto
Plummeted into/onto
Plunked oneself into/onto
Propelled oneself into/onto
Propped oneself on
Put down roots in/on
Put one's feet up

R
Relaxed in/on
Remained in/on
Reclined in/on
Reposed in/on
Rested in/on
Roosted in/on
Rooted oneself in/on

S
Settled into/onto
Sagged into/onto
Sank into/onto
Seized a seat/chair
Settled into/onto
Skulked in/on
Slept in/on
Slouched into/onto
Slumped into/onto
Snoozed in/on
Sprawled out in/on
Squatted on the edge of
Squeezed into/onto
Stationed oneself in/on
Straddled
Stretched out in/on
Submerged in/on
Swooned into/onto

T
Tarried in/on
Threw oneself into/onto

Took a load off
Took a pew
Took a seat
Took the weight off
Tucked into/onto
Tumbled into/onto
Tunneled into/onto

U
Unwound in/on

V
Vegged in/on

W
Waited in/on
Wilted into

Shake the Head

Too many headshakes in your WIP?

Shaking heads appear so often in fiction they sometimes make me shake my head in disbelief. Are you aware that in some areas of the world a headshake signals agreement? Some readers could interpret your character's body language as approval. Why not clarify your writing and leave no room for misinterpretation?

What motivates your character? A shaking head could indicate:

Amusement, anger, anguish, anxiety, confusion, contempt, defensiveness, disagreement, disappointment, disbelief, discouragement, doubt, exasperation, frustration, impatience, regret, relief, reluctance, resignation, skepticism, smugness, surprise, unease

Let's examine body language that shows these emotions.

Amusement
Elevated eyebrows
Playful shoves or nudging
Entertaining observations
Chuckling, snorting, or cackling

Anger
Pursed lips
Sneering and/or snarling
Running hands through hair
Invading another person's personal space

Anguish
Visible sweating
Clenched fists
Restless movements
Flinching at unexpected sounds

Anxiety
Pacing
Darting gaze
Rubbing one's arms
Biting nails or fiddling with an object like a pen

Confusion
Wrinkled nose
Scratching the head
Excessive swallowing
Contradictory statements

Contempt
Pinched lips
Mocking grin
Nose in the air
Lopsided curling of the lip

Defensiveness
Crossed arms
Sitting with locked ankles
Shoulders pulled close to the body
Hands in pockets or clutching a purse

Disagreement
Deep frown
Waving someone away
Shuffling backward a few steps
Questioning or disputing someone's statements

Disappointment
Biting the lip
Grinding teeth
Slumped posture
Hands clasped behind the back

Disbelief
Rapid blinking
Mumbling dialogue
Resting fingertips on chest or cheek
Covering the mouth with one palm

Discouragement
Trembling chin
Monotone voice
Lifeless eyes
Slumped posture

Doubt
Halting dialogue
Rocking on the heels
Lips pressed firmly together
Rubbing the back of one's neck

Exasperation
Tapping foot
Fake smile
Sharp tone
Narrowed eyes

Frustration
Cursing
Clenched jaw
Bared teeth
Slamming doors or throwing objects

Impatience
Rapid dialogue
Leaning forward
Drumming or tapping the fingers
Shifting weight from one foot to the other

Regret
Shivering or trembling
Hiding face with hair, scarf, or hat
Inability to meet someone's eyes
Verbal assurances that one will right the wrong

Relief
Unsteady legs
Trembling laughter
Bowing the head, as in prayer
Exhalation of pent-up breath

Reluctance
Tense posture
Stammering or stuttering
Made-up reasons for not doing something
Delaying an inordinate time before answering questions

Resignation
Picking at food
Staring at nothing
Poor personal grooming
Monosyllabic answers to questions

Skepticism
Cocked head
Simpering smirk
Lips pressed together
Disparaging remarks

Smugness
Chin held high
Erect posture
Puffed out chest
Authoritative voice

Surprise
Furrowed brow
Gaping mouth
Quick step backward
Staring at object or person that caused the surprise

Unease
Tremulous voice
Fidgeting with clothing
Not responding to questions
Distracted dialogue, not understanding what another person says

Let's try body language in a few examples.

Phil <u>shook his head</u>. "No, you can't go in there."

Why does Phil say that? Maybe his voice would reflect his emotional state.

Phil's tremulous voice squeaked, sending a ripple of unease up my spine. "No, you can't go in there."

Is he hiding something in a closet?

Phil gaped and took a quick step backward. "No, you can't go in there."

Perhaps he's angry.

Phil leaned toward me, so close I could smell the honey-garlic ribs he had for supper. "No, you can't go in there."

Ingrid shakes her head too.

Ingrid <u>shook her head</u>. "I never did that. He's lying."

Ingrid's dialogue is clear. She's denying something. Is the action beat required? If we need to show who's speaking, we could add a dialogue tag.

"I never did that," Ingrid said. "He's lying."

Do we need to show anger?

"I never did that." Ingrid sneered. "He's lying."

Maybe Ingrid is amused. Perhaps she did whatever she has been accused of.

Ingrid nudged Judy with one elbow. "I never did that." She chuckled. "He's lying."

More examples that rely on alternatives from the following list.

Rochelle <u>shook her head</u>. "I can't talk about that now."

Can we interject emotion without increasing word count? Yes.

Rochelle <u>moaned</u>. "I can't talk about that now."

A moan shows that Rochelle is suffering.

Rochelle <u>declined</u> my suggestion. "I can't talk about that now."

Now Rochelle is refusing to cooperate. Perhaps she's stubborn or prefers not to deal with the situation.

Exercises and story prompts.

Try to eliminate headshakes in the following. Replace with body language or alternatives from the list. Feel free to use them as story prompts.

1. I reviewed Jewel's performance report and <u>shook my head</u>. Three bad reports in a row. This employee-turned-mistress situation was out of hand.

But what could I do? One wrong move and she would [Insert creative scenario. Does Jewel have blackmail material? Is she pregnant? Does the boss need her because she's developing software only she is capable of maintaining? Maybe she has changed the passwords to all his offshore bank accounts.]

2. Brenda <u>shook her head,</u> reluctant to accompany the stranger. Sure, he said all the right words. He was good-looking. Yet, something about his eyes didn't seem right. When she gazed into them, she lost all sense of time and space.

3. Bill's elbow throbbed worse than a toothache. He <u>shook his head</u>. "You can't make me. I'm not hooked; honest I'm not. I can quit anytime I want. Just give me a chance." [What is he "not hooked" on? Why is his elbow throbbing?]

4. "Twenty-five years. I've stuck by you for twenty-five years." Zach <u>shook his head</u>. "Now you want me to give up everything I've ever worked for and [What is he supposed to give up and what is he expected to replace it with? A successful business exchanged for a two-person sailing trip around the world? A mansion for a cabin in the woods? A singing career for a doughnut shop?]"

The list of alternatives for *shake the head*.

Short alternatives will often *tell* rather than *show*. If your word count allows, try these as seeds for more extensive scenarios.

<u>A</u>
Abandon, abjure, abnegate, abrogate, abstain, argue, avert, avoid

B
Bail out, balk, bar, belie, block

C
Cancel, cavil, censure, challenge, clash, complain, condemn, confute, contradict, controvert, counter, counteract, countermand, criticize

D
Debate, decline, demur, deny, deter, deviate, differ, disaffirm, disagree, disapprove, disavow, disclaim, discountenance, disengage, dismiss, disprove, dissent, ditch, dodge, draw away, drop out, duck

E
Eschew, evade

F
Foil, forbid, forswear

G
Gainsay, get in the way, give a thumbs down, go against, gripe, grouse

H
Halt, hamper, hinder

I
Impede, impugn, interdict, invalidate

K
Kibosh, kill

M
Moan

N
Naysay, negate, nix, nullify

O
Object, obviate, oppose, oppugn, overrule, overturn

P
Pass up, prevent, prohibit, proscribe, protest, pull back

Q
Quail, quash, quell, quit

R
Raise objections, rebut, refrain, refuse, refute, reject, remonstrate, renege, renounce, repress, repudiate, rescind, resist, retract, retreat, reverse, revoke, rule out

S
Say no, scrap, scuttle, shoot down, speak against, spurn, squelch, steer clear of, stop, stymie, suppress

T
Take exception, take issue, thwart, turn down

U
Undermine

V
Veto, voice reservations

W
Ward off, withdraw

Shrug

Why do your characters shrug?

Perhaps you rely on shrugs as action beats to differentiate between speakers in dialogue; or maybe you're on an early draft, and you write the first thing that comes to mind.

A shrug should be more than an action beat. People shrug for many reasons. If you can determine their motivation, you can substitute alternative body language.

Some emotions that might cause a shrug include:

Confusion, deception, defensiveness, denial, determination, disbelief, doubt, indifference, insecurity, resignation, skepticism, sympathy, uncertainty, worry

Consider a few ways you could show these emotions.

Confusion
Rapid blinking
Rubbing the chin
Scratching the head
Wrinkling the nose

Deception
Shifty eyes
Lack of eye contact
Changing the subject
Hesitating when answering questions

Defensiveness
Squinting
Licking the lips
Leaning away from someone
Holding something in front of the body

Denial
Sweating
Shuffling backward
Locking eyes with someone
Raising the palms in a *not me* gesture

Determination
Hard jaw
Leaning forward
Cords or veins of neck standing out
Pressing on with an activity even if in pain or uncomfortable

Disbelief
Slack jaw
Wide eyes
Unfocused stare
Covering one's ears as though trying to block bad news

Doubt
Biting one's cheek
Avoidance of eye contact
Running fingers through hair
Rubbing the chin or the back of the neck

Indifference
Blank gaze
Speaking with hands in pockets
Turning away from someone who is speaking
Attention focused on other characters or objects

Insecurity
Forced smile
Biting nails or lips
Red face and upper torso
Fidgeting with hair or clothing

Resignation
Hanging head
Slumped shoulders
Trembling chin
Poor personal grooming

Skepticism
Mumbling
Rubbing the eyes
Unrestrained smirk
Tsk-tsking through crooked mouth

Sympathy
Stroking someone's hair
Fumbling/at a loss for words
Speaking in a soothing voice
Patting someone's back or hugging them

Uncertainty
Pacing
Halting dialogue
Puckered forehead
Repeated swallowing

Worry
Thin smile
Trembling
Dark circles under eyes
Thumbs clenched inside fists

Practical application.

Let's review how we could include appropriate body language in a few short passages.

Dale <u>*shrugged*</u>*. "I don't know what happened. One minute Hayley was smiling at me, and the next thing I knew, my shirt was drenched with the glass of wine she threw on me."*

Why did Dale shrug? Was he confused? Consumed by disbelief? Let's assume both.

"I don't know what happened." Dale blinked. "One minute Hayley was smiling at me," he continued, his eyes wide with disbelief, "and the next thing I knew, my shirt was drenched with the glass of wine she threw on me."

The second version contains a few more words, but it provides a better visual of Dale's reaction.

Ready for another?

Irene <u>shrugged</u>. Ten days since the interview, and still no callback.

Is Irene worried? Perhaps she has accepted what she considers the predictable result of a bad interview.

Irene flipped her greasy hair out of her face and scraped at a dried blob of ketchup on her pajamas. Ten days since the interview, and still no callback.

Her poor personal grooming is a good indication she has resigned herself to the inevitable.

What about Wade in the next example?

Wade <u>shrugged</u>. "That'll never work, you doorknob!"

Wade's dialogue shows his skepticism. However, if you need an action beat, how about something like the following?

Wade's smirk stretched so wide he looked like a rude caricature of the Cheshire Cat. "That'll never work, you doorknob!"

Review this list for more alternatives.

Many of the following will *tell* rather than *show*, which isn't always a taboo.

<u>A</u>
Apologize

<u>B</u>
Belittle, brush aside, brush off

<u>C</u>
Criticize

<u>D</u>
Defy, delay, denigrate, deride, disdain, dismiss, disobey, disparage, disregard

<u>E</u>
Express regret

<u>F</u>
Face-palm

<u>G</u>
Give the cold shoulder, goad

<u>H</u>
Hesitate

<u>I</u>
Ignore, insult

<u>J</u>
Jeer

<u>M</u>
Make light of, mock

<u>O</u>
Overlook

<u>P</u>
Pause, pay no attention to, pay no mind, plead ignorance, pooh-pooh, procrastinate, provoke

<u>R</u>
Rebuff, ridicule

<u>S</u>
Scoff, scorn, simper, slouch, sneer, snigger, snort, snub, stick out the tongue

<u>T</u>
Taunt, tease, twitch

V
Vacillate, vilify

W
Wring the hands

A final set of practical examples:

Bobby <u>shrugged</u> when Mommy told him to clean his room.

Lukewarm. Can we make his reaction stronger?

Mommy told Bobby to clean his room. He ignored her, continuing to play with his new video game.

We could give Bobby some attitude and set him up for a timeout or grounding.

When Mommy told Bobby to clean his room, he stuck out his tongue.

Time to revisit Hayley.

Hayley <u>shrugged</u>. "I'm sorry, Dale. I didn't mean to throw the glass of wine at you. It just slipped out of my hand and launched itself into the air, you insensitive jerk."

Using *apologize* as a verb wouldn't work. Although Hayley says she's sorry, she doesn't mean it. This might be a good place for a facial expression that shows her true emotions.

"I'm sorry, Dale," Hayley said. Her ensuing simper sent all the bystanders into a cacophony of nervous giggles and outright guffaws. "I didn't mean to throw the glass of wine at you. It just slipped out of my hand and launched itself into the air, you insensitive jerk."

Do you *need* an action beat or dialogue tag?

Excellent dialogue should be able to stand on its own. If you make it clear who's talking, untagged speech often speeds the narrative.

Dale <u>shrugged</u>. "It's all right."

Hayley <u>shrugged</u> back. "Really?"

"Sure," Dale replied. "I own three drycleaners and twenty men's clothing stores."

"Well in that case," Hayley said as she threw the rest of the wine at him, "let's keep them in business."

The two main characters in this scene are Dale and Hayley. There's no reason to repeat their names. Once we know who's talking, we don't need to re-establish their identities in every paragraph.

Time for a rewrite to eliminate the shrugs and add some detail.

Dale sneered. "It's all right."

"Really?" Hayley squinted at him.

"Sure. I own three drycleaners and twenty men's clothing stores."

"Well in that case, let's keep them in business." She sploshed the entire bottle of wine over his Armani suit, Rolex watch, and Berluti shoes.

Better?

Try these story prompts.

Remove all instances of *shrugged* in the following, developing them into micro-fiction or longer stories.

1. The policeman <u>shrugged</u>. Three robberies at the same jewelry store in the last week, and now a fourth?

2. No time like the present. Muhammed <u>shrugged</u>. It was now or never.

3. Francine stared at her reflection in the full-length mirror. She <u>shrugged</u>. White had never been her favorite color.

4. The loud argument in the neighboring apartment ceased as abruptly as it had begun. Harold <u>shrugged</u>. Another night, another spat. When would they ever—

A sharp crack decimated the blessed silence.

5. Twenty-four balloons. Not twenty-three. Not twenty-five. One for each time Tod had asked. He <u>shrugged</u>. Was he destined to reach twenty-five?

6. "I can't do this," Helen said.

Maxwell <u>shrugged</u> as he pushed her. "Sure you can. Look. You just did."

She screamed.

7. Bernie's white-knuckled fingers clung to the steering wheel. He <u>shrugged</u>. "I swear, officer, I was going five under the speed limit."

"More like fifty over, sonny boy." The cop <u>shrugged</u>. "But I could be persuaded to ferget this. Ten bucks fer each mile over should do it, I reckon."

Bernie reached for [Choose or invent a phrase: the glove compartment, his gun, his wallet, his cell phone, a breath mint, the GPS, the map light.]

8. Freddy <u>shrugged</u>. "I wasn't cheating, Miss Martin, honest I wasn't."

She glowered at him. "Then why were you staring over Susan's shoulder?"

"Because she has my cell phone, and [zany excuse]."

Sigh

Uh-oh. You just reviewed your novel and found over one hundred instances of *sighed*. Aargh! How can you fix your story without a major rewrite?

Before we begin, consider this.

Have you ever tried to laugh, hiss, or sigh while you're talking? Try it.

Now, scrutinize the following sentence.

He sighed, "You're impossible."

Note that *He sighed* has been used as a dialogue tag. But you can't sigh dialogue.

Correct:

He sighed. "You're impossible."

Here, *He sighed* is changed into an action beat by replacing the comma with a period.

Now that's out of the way, let's contemplate how to remove all those duplicate *sighs* in your writing.

Motivation is key.

If you don't know the reason behind your character's sigh, how can you expect your readers to? They're not telepathic.

Review the following emotions that might cause a sigh:

Adulation, agitation, compassion, cynicism, delight, exasperation, failure, impatience, loneliness, longing, overconfidence, remorse, resolve, self-doubt, stoicism, suspense, suspicion, tranquility

Consider some of the available alternatives.

Adulation
Moistening of the lips
Adjusting/smoothing clothing
Following someone with the eyes
Nodding at everything a person says

Agitation
Pacing
Scowling
Chewing on nails/lips
Glancing at a door or wristwatch

Compassion
Nodding
Embracing someone
Leaning toward someone
Speaking words of comfort in a soft tone

Cynicism
Smirking
Twisted sneer
Pursing the lips
Glaring in a condescending manner

Delight
Grinning
Whistling
Giving a fist bump or thumbs-up
Wrinkles at the corners of the eyes

Exasperation
Clenching the fists
Shaking the head
Snarls and sneers
Pointing a finger at someone

Failure
Slouching
Hunched posture
Staring at one's feet
Staring with vacant expression

Impatience
Pinched lips
Slamming doors
Throwing objects
Shifting weight from foot to foot

Loneliness
Repressing tears
Neglecting personal grooming
Spending an inordinate time with pets
Long hours surfing the internet or playing video games

Longing
Flushed skin
Biting one's bottom lip
Leaning toward someone
Gazing into the distance with a faraway expression

Overconfidence
Puffed-out chest
Sneering or smirking
Bellowing in an authoritative voice
Standing with feet spread wide and crossed arms

Remorse
Slumping shoulders
Squeezing eyes shut
Cupping the mouth with hands
Wincing as memories or shame surface

Resolve
Thin lips
Firming the jaw
Assuming an aggressive posture
Reacting with strong movements

Self-doubt
Biting one's lip
Mumbling
Shuffling feet
Excessive swallowing

<u>Stoicism</u>
Trembling chin
Hiding physical pain
Losing one's appetite
Speaking in a toneless voice

<u>Suspense</u>
Sweating
Fidgeting with hands
Playing with hair or mustache
Reacting with fluttering heart and racing pulse

<u>Suspicion</u>
Tight smile
Grinding teeth
Refusing assistance
Stuffing hands into pockets or fiddling with purse

<u>Tranquility</u>
Humming
Relaxed posture
Slow, even breathing
Greeting everyone on the street

Would dialogue work better?

If your character's sigh is not just an action beat but a means to communicate emotion, dialogue might be your answer. Sometimes a well-worded snippet of conversation will say more than an entire paragraph of action beats and body language.

<u>Adulation</u>
"Nobody does it better."
"Roses, just for you."
"You're the most perfect woman a guy could ever ask for."

<u>Agitation</u>
"Humph."
"You'll be the death of me yet."
"What's the matter with you, you incompetent boob?"

Compassion
"Aww. I understand."
"I feel your pain."
"I wish it could have been me instead."

Cynicism
"Meh."
"You can lead a horse to water, but ..."
"Yeah, I'll wait. It's not like I have anything important to do."

Delight
"For me? Really? I can't believe it!"
"It's Friday. Friday!"
"Of course! Why didn't I see the answer sooner?"

Exasperation
"Aargh!"
"No, no, no, no, NO!"
"If I've told you once, I've told you a million times ..."

Failure
"I'll never figure this out."
"I'll resign in the morning."
"Burnt. Again. Cooking was never my strong point."

Impatience
"Hurry up. We don't have all day, you slowpoke."
"No, I don't need your help. Not enough time in the day."
"Forget the dessert. We have to leave as soon as we get the bill."

Loneliness
"Nobody gives a hoot what an old lady thinks."
"I feel isolated, like a prisoner in solitary confinement."
"You don't know what lonely is until you've spent a decade eating breakfast with a cat as your only company."

Longing
"If only I could ..."
"What if ..."
"Ah, the old days. People don't know what they're missing."

Overconfidence

"I can beat you anytime, anywhere."

"He doesn't know beans. Leave it to me."

"I got what you need, baby. And lots of it. XL."

Remorse

"I'm so, so sorry."

"If only I could do it all over again ..."

"One million, two; how much will it take to pay for my mistake?"

Resolve

"Come on. We can do this."

"Everything is possible if you give it enough time."

"No matter what he does or how much he insults me, I refuse to cry."

Self-doubt

"I can't fight them alone. I just can't."

"I'm not sure. I've never done this before."

"But the last time I tried this, it was a colossal flop."

Suspense

"Are we there yet?"

"... and? Get to the end of the story before I wet myself."

"C'mon, tell me. Who did you invite for supper? Your mother?"

Suspicion

"Are you really a movie producer?"

"I hardly know you. Can I bring a friend along with me?"

"Nobody else could have done it. You were the only person in the room."

Tranquility

"Ah! This is the life."

"Me? Worry? That word isn't even in my vocabulary."

"Fuzzy slippers, a glass of wine, and a good book. Perfect."

More action beats you could use to replace sighs:

- Face plant

- Fake smile

- Finger stroking or tapping the chin

- Gritting one's teeth

- Head in one's hands

- Rolling the eyes

- Shaking the head

- Shrugging

- Staring out the window

- Steepled fingers

Here's a list of direct replacements for *sigh*.

Determine your character's motivation. Then, pick a verb from the following list or search for something similar in your favorite thesaurus.

A
Ache, agonize

B
Bark, bellow, bemoan, bewail, blare, blat, blub, blubber, bray, breathe, brood

C
Cackle, carp, caterwaul, chafe, choke, clamor, cluck, complain, crave

D
Declaim, decry

E
Effuse, exhale

F
Fret

G
Gasp, gripe, groan, grouse, growl, grumble, grunt, gulp, gurgle

H
Hanker, hiccup, hiss, howl, huff

I
Inhale

K
Keen

L
Lament, languish, long for

M
Meditate, mewl, moan, mope, mumble, muse, mutter

O
Obsess

P
Pant, pine, pout, puff, pule, purr

R
Reflect, rue

S
Sibilate, snap, snarl, sneeze, sniff, sniffle, snivel, snort, snuffle, sob, sough, spew a gasp of frustration, squall, squawk, squeal, stew, sulk, suspire

T
Thirst

U
Utter a popping hiss of anger

W
Wail, wheeze, whimper, whine, whistle

Y
Yammer, yawp, yowl

Think

I think you're probably reading this chapter because you think you can learn to decrease your reliance on the word *think* in your writing. Am I right? I think I can help.

Effective formatting removes the need for *think*.

In the old days when a character had a thought, the writer might have penned something like this:

1. Aaron sighed. "The sins of the fathers," he <u>thought</u>, "always return to haunt their children." His fist drove into the wall and created a gaping hole.

Some writers still use this type of construction.

However, quotation marks, which usually introduce dialogue, can be misinterpreted if you also use them for internal monologue.

The previous example doesn't become clear until a person reaches *he thought*. Why confuse your readers?

Other writers might punctuate like this:

2. Aaron sighed. The sins of the fathers, he <u>thought</u>, always return to haunt their children. His fist drove into the wall and created a gaping hole.

Removing the quotation marks clarifies somewhat. However, a reader might expect a narrative statement in the second sentence.

Italics can obviate the need for *he thought*.

3. Aaron sighed. *The sins of the fathers always return to haunt their children.* His fist drove into the wall and created a gaping hole.

How many instances of *think* and its inflections could you remove with the italics approach?

Be careful, though. Overuse of italics can distract readers. Longer passages can be handled like this:

4. Aaron sighed. The sins of the fathers always returned to haunt their children. His fist drove into the wall and created a gaping hole.

The preceding excerpt reports Aaron's thoughts indirectly. Because the passage is written from his point of view, readers will understand that the second sentence reflects his personal opinion.

This is the best approach for anything longer than a sentence or two.

Review all your verbs, not just *think*.

Sometimes your character needs to think without revealing specific thoughts.

1. The teacher sat in the chair and <u>thought</u> gloomily while she graded papers. [13 words]

The sentence is lukewarm and uses a much-maligned adverb. Does the next one work better?

2. The teacher slumped in the chair and <u>brooded</u> while she graded papers. [12 words]

Or consider this version:

3. The teacher perched on her chair and <u>daydreamed</u> while she graded papers. [12 words]

Active verbs paint different pictures and strengthen your writing.

Dialogue is an effective tool.

Well-written dialogue breathes new life into a piece if you choose different words for *think*. Consider these sentences:

1. "I <u>think</u> the victim died from an overdose."

2. "I <u>posit</u> the victim died from an overdose."

The first sentence could have been said by just about anyone. The second is more likely to have come from a forensic anthropologist like Dr. Temperance Brennan from *Bones.*

Never, never, never; uh, uh; no, no.

What's wrong with the next sentence?

1. You're not my boss, John thought to himself.

Answer: *Think* is not a reflexive verb. Who or what else would John be thinking to? The wife who just nagged him about mowing the lawn? His big toe?

Chop the last part:

2. You're not my boss, John thought.

The following phrases can replace *I think*.

- As far as I can tell

- As far as I'm concerned

- As I see it

- I assume

- I believe

- I consider

- I guess

- I suppose

- I would say

- In my opinion

- In my point of view

- It seems to me that

- It's my belief that

- It's my view that

- The way I see it

- To my way of thinking

Here's the list.

<u>A</u>
Agonize, analyze, apperceive, apply one's mind, appraise, appreciate, ascertain, assess, assume

<u>B</u>
Be certain of, be convinced of, be credulous, be of the opinion, believe, brainstorm, brood, buy

<u>C</u>
Calculate, cerebrate, chew over, cogitate, comprehend, conceive, concentrate, conceptualize, conclude, concoct, conjecture, conjure up, consider, construe, contemplate, contrive, cook up

<u>D</u>
Daydream, debate, decipher, deduce, deem, deliberate, demur, determine, devise, digest, discern, dissect, dither, divine, dwell upon

<u>E</u>
Equivocate, evaluate, envisage, envision, entertain a thought, establish, estimate, evaluate, evoke, examine, excogitate, expect, extrapolate

<u>F</u>
Fabricate, fancy, fantasize, fathom, feel, figure, find, flash on, focus, form an opinion, form ideas, formulate, free-associate, fret, fuss

<u>G</u>
Gather, gauge, get, get an idea, give credence to, glean, grasp, guess, guesstimate

<u>H</u>
Hallucinate, hanker, hash over, hatch, have a flash, have a hunch, have a notion, have a vision, have in mind, have no doubt, hazard a guess, hope, hypothesize

I
Ideate, imagine, infer, intellectualize, interpret, introspect, intuit, invent

J
Judge

K
Know

M
Maintain, mean, meditate, mull, muse

O
Opine, originate

P
Perceive, percolate, perpend, philosophize, picture, plan, plot, ponder, posit, postulate, predicate, predict, presume, presuppose, prevaricate, propose, propound, puzzle over

R
Ratiocinate, rationalize, read, realize, reason, recall, reckon, recognize, reflect, regard, rehash, repine, resolve, ruminate

S
Scheme, scrutinize, sense, sort out, speculate, stargaze, stew, suppose, surmise, suspect, sweat over, syllogize

T
Take in, theorize, thresh out, toy with an idea, trust, twig

U
Understand, use one's head

V
Vacillate, view, visualize

W
Waffle, weigh, wonder, woolgather, work out, worry

Turn

Woot! Your WIP is now a novel.

The first chapter whispers, "Come here. I'm ready for my initial round of edits."

You respond.

Your WIP groans with every deletion, addition, and grammar correction.

Unease creeps into your fingertips. You reread the first ten pages. Aargh! Fourteen repetitions of *turned*.

What next?

Let's analyze why you might choose *turn*. We'll start with Google's definition: "move or cause to move in a circular direction wholly or partly around an axis or point."

A turn can be a change in direction or emotion. And remember, a person can turn toward, not just away.

Why would someone turn?

If you know what drives a character, you can substitute alternative body language or reactions.

"What's my motivation?" an actor might ask before performing. Without an understanding of the impetus behind actions in each scene, the performance could come across as unrealistic.

The following emotions might result in a full or partial turn.

Agitation, confusion, contempt, deceit, defense, disapproval, disbelief, embarrassment, fear, disinterest, frustration, guilt, indifference, modesty, protection, reluctance, sadness, scorn, smugness, social anxiety

Consider the information below each underlined word to see a few different ways you could express it.

Agitation
Nail-biting
Tapping foot
Sweaty palms
Drumming fingers

Confusion
Shifty eyes
Frowning
Wrinkling the nose
Scratching or cocking the head

Contempt
Sneer
Crossed arms
Wrinkled nose
Eyebrows drawn together

Deceit
Lying
Stuttering
Balled up hands
Chewing the inside of the cheek

Defense
Clenched fists
Hands in pockets
Sitting with crossed ankles
Holding something, like a drink, in front of the body

Disapproval
Blinking
Clenched jaw
Flared nostrils
Rubbing the eyes

Disbelief
Pursed lips
Dropped jaw
Rubbing the nose
Scratching the neck

Embarrassment
Slumping
Trembling
Nail-biting
Massaging the forehead

Fear
Recoiling
Wide eyes
Tense lips
Elevated heart rate

Disinterest
Straying glance
Lack of eye contact
Nonchalant stance
Inspecting fingernails

Frustration
Teeth grinding
Kicking a tire or wall
Thumbs clenched inside fists
Hands clasped behind the back

Guilt
False smile
Changing topic
Grimace or blush
Avoidance of eye contact

Indifference
No laughing at jokes
Leaning away from speaker
Minimal response to conversation
Constantly checking phone or watch

Modesty
Fidgeting
Chewing on lip
Blushing and glancing away
Covering with arms or clothing

Protection (from weather, bomb blast, speeding vehicle, etc.)
Flinching
Diving to the ground
Fleeing the scene
Shielding head or body with arms

Reluctance
Cleaning glasses
Fiddling with hair
Tugging on an ear
Fingers tapping chin

Sadness
Tears
Lowering of head
Slumped posture
Downturned mouth

Scorn
Snort
Curled lip
Nose in the air
Throbbing vein in forehead

Smugness
Aloof manner
Puffed-out chest
Authoritative voice
Trying to hide a smirk

Social anxiety
Fidgeting
Hugging oneself
Clearing the throat
Retreating into a quiet room

A person might turn to hide:

- A black eye or facial bruising (embarrassment)

- Breastfeeding (modesty, social anxiety)

- Chocolate on the chin (deceit)

- Clumsily applied lipstick or mascara (embarrassment)

- A festering pimple (embarrassment, social anxiety)

- A missing tooth (embarrassment, social anxiety)

- Body piercing such as a ring in the nose (deceit, embarrassment)

- The smell of cigarettes on the breath (deceit)

- Spinach in the teeth (embarrassment)

What could a character do instead of turning? Would any of the previously mentioned actions work?

Stand in front of a mirror and pretend you're an actor. How else could you show the same emotions?

Do you need direct replacements for *turn*?

You might find what you need in the following list.

Experiment with the words. Some can show emotion as well as movement. For example, a truck driver faced with a decision might change course or reverse direction. Embrace double meanings.

A
About-face, avoid

B
Back off, backpedal, backtrack, bypass

C
Cartwheel, change course, change direction, circumvent, coil, come about, corkscrew, curve left/right

D
Detour, diverge, do a one-eighty/three-sixty, dodge, double back

E
Edge around, elude, evade

F
Face about, flee, flip

G
Gee, go home, go the other way, gyrate, gyre

H
Hang a left/right, haw, head back, hesitate

L
Loop around, lurch

M
Make a one-eighty, make an about-face, make a left/right, meander, merge left/right

O
Orbit, oscillate

P
Pirouette, pivot

R
Reel, retrace one's steps, retreat, return, reverse course, reverse direction, revolve, roll left/right, rotate

S
Show one's back, sidestep, snake, snap around, spin, spiral, steer left/right, sweep around, swerve, swing around, swirl, swivel

T
Take a left/right, thread, twine, twirl, twist, twizzle

U
U-ey, u-turn

V
Veer, volte-face

W

Wander away, weave, wend left/right, wheel about, whip around, whirl about, wind

Y

Yaw

Z

Zig-zag

Very

Are you very aware of the very prolific advice from very erudite sources telling you to be very wary of using *very* in your writing? I'm very happy to say I'm very willing to help with the following very extensive list of ways to avoid *very*.

Do you see what happened in the previous paragraph? I used *very* so many times, nine, to be exact, that it lost its emphasis—an excellent example of the type of writing to avoid.

You should delete most, if not all, instances of this frowned-upon word. The rest of the time, you can usually find a single word that works better than the original phrase.

If *very* is a misdemeanor, a double instance of the word is a very, very big felony. Rather than emphasizing, the repetition dilutes the power of your prose.

Sorry, you won't fool your readers with substitutes such as *really, truly, genuinely, sincerely, exceedingly, especially, truthfully, thoroughly,* and their relatives.

Is your female protagonist really angry? Why not say she is *furious*? What about your male protagonist who is especially strong? You can call him *brawny* or *powerful*.

Exception to the rule: In dialogue, anything goes. People often use slang and incorrect grammar when speaking. If you want your characters to breathe on the page, their speech should sound realistic.

Instead of modifying with *very*, try the suggested alternatives in the following list.

P.S. If you're having a very difficult time removing *very* from your writing, remember Mark Twain's advice: "Substitute 'damn' every time you're inclined to write 'very'; your editor will delete it, and the writing will be just as it should be."

Using the first row as an example, if you wish to say *very accurate*, instead try *precise, exact, unimpeachable, perfect,* or *flawless.*

Accurate ...... precise, exact, unimpeachable, perfect, flawless

Aggressive ...... forceful, assertive, overconfident, hardline

Amazed ...... astounded, flabbergasted, astonished, shocked

Angry, mad ...... furious, irate, enraged, incensed, fuming, livid

Antagonistic ...... hostile, incompatible, militant, pugnacious

Anxious ...... dismayed, apprehensive, restless, fretful

Approving ...... effusive, unrestrained, gushy, fulsome

Ashamed ...... abashed, sheepish, disconcerted, discomposed

Assertive ...... emphatic, overbearing, overconfident, arrogant

Aware ...... conscious, savvy, apprised, mindful, cognizant

Awkward ...... clumsy, uncoordinated, graceless, maladroit

Bad ...... awful, deplorable, appalling, rotten, miserable

Basic ...... rudimentary, primary, fundamental, simple

Beautiful ...... gorgeous, stunning, exquisite, magnificent

Bitter ...... rancorous, acrimonious, disenchanted

Bloody ...... gory, brutal, barbarous, savage, murderous

Blurry ...... indistinct, nebulous, unclear, obscure, hazy

Bony ...... skeletal, angular, spindly, gaunt, emaciated

Borderline ...... unclassifiable, indeterminate, ambiguous, iffy

Boring ...... tedious, dreary, uninteresting, mind-numbing

Bright ...... brilliant, dazzling, radiant, blinding, intense

Busy ...... swamped, diligent, industrious, harried

Callous ...... ruthless, inhumane, merciless, heartless

Capable ...... efficient, competent, adept, proficient, skillful

Careful ...... meticulous, fastidious, precise, scrupulous

Caring ...... compassionate, kind, attentive, sympathetic

Careless ...... negligent, haphazard, sloppy, irresponsible, lax

Chagrined ...... displeased, annoyed, bothered, irked, peeved

Civil ...... polite, courteous, respectful, cultured, mannerly

Clean ...... spotless, immaculate, stainless, hygienic

Clear ...... transparent, sheer, translucent, glassy, crystal

Clever ...... astute, brilliant, shrewd, ingenious, crafty, sharp

Cold ...... frigid, bitter, icy, freezing, glacial, frosty, polar

Colorful ...... vibrant, vivid, kaleidoscopic, variegated, vivid

Committed ...... unshakeable, unswerving, wholehearted

Competitive ...... ambitious, driven, cutthroat, bloodthirsty

Concerned ...... worried, troubled, upset, distressed, agitated

Confident ...... poised, cool, self-assured, self-reliant, secure

<u>Confused</u> ...... baffled, befuddled, mystified, clueless, dazed

<u>Confusing</u> ...... incomprehensible, unintelligible, indecipherable

<u>Conscious</u> ...... deliberate, intentional, premeditated, willful

<u>Consistent</u> ...... constant, unfailing, uniform, harmonious, same

<u>Contrary</u> ...... belligerent, argumentative, confrontational

<u>Conventional</u> ...... conservative, common, predictable, unoriginal

<u>Cordial</u> ...... affable, genial, gracious, convivial

<u>Corrupt</u> ...... fraudulent, crooked, unethical, dishonest, rotten

<u>Creamy</u> ...... velvety, buttery, rich, smooth, milky, greasy

<u>Creepy</u> ...... unnerving, skin-crawling, spooky, sinister

<u>Critical</u> ...... vital, crucial, essential, indispensable, integral

<u>Crude</u> ...... unrefined, obscene, indecent, churlish

<u>Crunchy</u> ...... crispy, brittle, crackling, gravelly, crusty, gritty

<u>Curious</u> ...... inquisitive, nosy, prying, snoopy, quizzical

<u>Cute</u> ...... adorable, endearing, delightful, pretty

<u>Dangerous</u> ...... perilous, precarious, unsafe, treacherous, dicey

<u>Dark</u> ...... black, inky, ebony, sooty, lightless, starless

<u>Deceitful</u> ...... false, duplicitous, devious, underhanded

<u>Decent</u> ...... civilized, upright, courteous, respectable, noble

<u>Deep</u> ...... abysmal, bottomless, cavernous, yawning, vast

<u>Deformed</u> ...... twisted, contorted, misshapen, mutilated

<u>Delicate</u> ...... subtle, slight, fragile, frail, flimsy, insubstantial

<u>Desperate</u> ...... frantic, fraught, grave, serious, hopeless, dire

<u>Despondent</u> ...... crestfallen, glum, doleful, woebegone, plaintive

<u>Determined</u> ...... resolute, adamant, obstinate, tenacious, dogged

<u>Different</u> ...... unusual, distinctive, atypical, dissimilar, unlike

<u>Difficult</u> ...... complicated, complex, demanding, arduous

<u>Diligent</u> ...... thorough, painstaking, indefatigable, particular

<u>Dirty</u> ...... filthy, foul, grimy, polluted, squalid, dilapidated

<u>Disagreeable</u> ...... contrary, obnoxious, offensive, repugnant, rude

<u>Disconcerting</u> ...... alarming, disheartening, bewildering, unnerving

<u>Disheartened</u> ...... demoralized, discouraged, daunted, dispirited

<u>Disheartening</u> ...... soul-crushing, shattering, overwhelming

<u>Dismal</u> ...... miserable, cheerless, depressing, morbid

<u>Distinct</u> ...... clear, definite, patent, evident, apparent

<u>Disturbing</u> ...... ominous, upsetting, terrifying, heinous, ghastly

<u>Dramatic</u> ...... theatrical, histrionic, melodramatic, vivid

<u>Dry</u> ...... arid, parched, sere, dehydrated, withered

<u>Dubious</u> ...... suspicious, skeptical, cynical, unconvinced

<u>Dull(1)</u> ...... monotonous, insipid, banal, mundane, stale

<u>Dull(2)</u> ...... drab, dingy, gloomy, lackluster, dim, murky

Eager ...... impatient, ardent, fervent, keen, earnest
Early ...... premature, preliminary, too soon, unexpected
Easy ...... effortless, uncomplicated, unchallenging
Educational ...... enlightening, edifying, informative, revealing
Efficient ...... competent, proficient, resourceful, able
Embarrassed ...... mortified, humiliated, discomfited, ashamed
Emotional ...... demonstrative, sensitive, temperamental
Enthusiastic ...... zealous, eager, fervent, vehement, ebullient
Exciting ...... exhilarating, electrifying, thrilling, breathtaking
Expensive ...... costly, exorbitant, overpriced, extravagant
Fair ...... equitable, impartial, neutral, nonpartisan
Faithful ...... loyal, devoted, staunch, unwavering, stalwart
Familiar ...... common, established, typical, traditional
Famous ...... renowned, eminent, legendary, celebrated
Far ...... distant, remote, isolated, secluded, extrasolar
Fast ...... rapid, swift, fleet, blistering, supersonic
Fat ...... obese, corpulent, rotund, blubbery, round
Fertile ...... prolific, productive, fruitful, rich, lush, fecund
Few ...... meager, scarce, scant, limited, negligible
Fierce ...... vicious, ferocious, savage, keen, intense, feral
Firm ...... solid, hard, rigid, set, frozen, unyielding
Fizzy ...... effervescent, frothy, foamy, sudsy
Fluffy ...... downy, fuzzy, fleecy, feathery, cottony
Focused ...... absorbed, fixated, riveted, engrossed
Fond ...... devoted, attentive, enamored, doting
Foolish ...... absurd, preposterous, ludicrous, irrational, daft
Fragile ...... tenuous, unstable, precarious, frail, delicate
Friendly ...... gregarious, outgoing, chummy, demonstrative
Frustrating ...... exasperating, infuriating, disheartening, vexing
Fulfilling ...... worthwhile, meaningful, empowering
Full ...... overflowing, bursting, crammed, packed, sated
Funny ...... hilarious, hysterical, sidesplitting, rollicking
Gentle ...... tender, mild, mellow, soothing, softhearted
Good ...... superb, superior, excellent, outstanding
Graceful ...... flowing, supple, lithe, willowy, lissome
Grateful ...... obliged, indebted, beholden, gratified, relieved
Greedy ...... gluttonous, avaricious, materialistic, insatiable
Hairy ...... hirsute, shaggy, furry, bushy, unshaven
Handsome ...... striking, suave, hunky, mesmeric, dynamite
Happy ...... ecstatic, overjoyed, euphoric, blissful, elated
Hard ...... inflexible, stony, steely, unyielding, tough, rigid

Healthy ...... hale, hardy, flourishing, fit, robust, vigorous
Heavy ...... leaden, ponderous, weighty, dense, hefty
Helpful ...... supportive, obliging, invaluable
Hesitant ...... indecisive, loath, reluctant, averse, disinclined
Honest ...... candid, sincere, authentic, forthright, frank
Horrible ...... atrocious, unspeakable, vile, abominable
Hot ...... burning, scalding, blistering, scorching, searing
Humble ...... meek, unpretentious, unassuming, obsequious
Hungry ...... starving, famished, ravenous, hollow, voracious
Ill ...... infirm, bedridden, frail, terminal, incurable
Immature ...... childish, infantile, naive, jejune, callow, green
Immoral ...... depraved, decadent, debauched, iniquitous
Impatient ...... restive, agog, uptight, disquieted, testy
Impertinent ...... brazen, impolite, brash, impudent, unmannerly
Important ...... crucial, vital, essential, paramount, imperative
Impressive ...... extraordinary, remarkable, awe-inspiring
Industrious ...... assiduous, unflagging, persevering, punctilious
Inebriated ...... intoxicated, drunk, soused, smashed, plastered
Informal ...... casual, unceremonious, easygoing, simple
Ingratiating ...... sycophantic, fawning, smarmy, servile
Insensitive ...... tactless, thoughtless, undiplomatic, blunt, crass
Insincere ...... artificial, hypocritical, mendacious, phony
Intelligent ...... brainy, clever, bright, gifted, intellectual, astute
Intense ...... severe, extreme, fierce, overpowering, acute
Interesting ...... fascinating, remarkable, riveting, compelling
Irritating ...... abrasive, trying, galling, irksome, maddening
Itchy ...... skin-crawling, tingly, prickly, tickling
Jealous ...... envious, resentful, grudging, green, bitter
Jovial ...... joyous, jubilant, bubbly, sunny, blithe
Juicy ...... succulent, moist, ripe, luscious, fleshy, syrupy
Laborious ...... grueling, exhausting, debilitating, punishing
Large ...... huge, humongous, mammoth, gargantuan
Lasting ...... timeless, everlasting, perennial, abiding, ageless
Late ...... last-minute, belated, delayed, eleventh-hour
Lavish ...... excessive, opulent, posh, luxurious, sumptuous
Lazy ...... apathetic, lackadaisical, indolent, unmotivated
Light ...... buoyant, insubstantial, weightless, airy, ethereal
Likely ...... expected, imminent, probable, unavoidable
Limited ...... constrained, restricted, insufficient, inadequate
Limp ...... lifeless, flaccid, wilted, shriveled, quaggy
Lively ...... energetic, vivacious, exuberant, spirited

<u>Logical</u> ...... rational, cogent, credible, consistent, sound
<u>Lonely</u> ...... isolated, deserted, forlorn, solitary, abandoned
<u>Long</u> ...... extended, extensive, interminable, protracted
<u>Loud</u> ...... deafening, thunderous, booming, blaring
<u>Loved</u> ...... adored, precious, cherished, revered, beloved
<u>Lucky</u> ...... charmed, blessed, favored, fortunate, fluky
<u>Manipulative</u> ...... cunning, wily, calculating, tricky, sneaky
<u>Many</u> ...... countless, innumerable, incalculable, untold
<u>Moody</u> ...... morose, temperamental, unstable, changeable
<u>Much</u> ...... plenty, oceans, heaps, scads, oodles, loads
<u>Much so</u> ...... of course, okay, yes, absolutely, precisely
<u>Musical</u> ...... melodic, melodious, harmonious, dulcet
<u>Near</u> ...... handy, close-by, alongside, convenient, nearby
<u>Neat</u> ...... orderly, tidy, uncluttered, immaculate, spotless
<u>Necessary</u> ...... compulsory, mandatory, top-priority, must-have
<u>Negative</u> ...... pessimistic, defeatist, cynical, critical, fatalistic
<u>New</u> ...... novel, innovative, fresh, original, cutting-edge
<u>Nice</u> ...... enjoyable, pleasant, agreeable, satisfying
<u>Nonplussed</u> ...... speechless, thunderstruck, stumped, unnerved
<u>Numerous</u> ...... abundant, copious, myriad, profuse
<u>Obvious</u> ...... apparent, clear, evident, plain, visible
<u>Occasionally</u> ...... seldom, rarely, infrequently, sporadically
<u>Old</u> ...... grizzled, aged, hoary, ancient, grey, decrepit
<u>Offended</u> ...... appalled, disgusted, outraged, revolted
<u>Old-fashioned</u> ...... obsolete, obsolescent, dated, outmoded
<u>Opinionated</u> ...... dogmatic, cocksure, biased, partisan
<u>Optimistic</u> ...... enthusiastic, buoyant, encouraged, positive
<u>Painful</u> ...... excruciating, agonizing, searing, unbearable
<u>Pale</u> ...... white, pallid, ashen, sallow, colorless, pasty
<u>Peaceful</u> ...... serene, tranquil, placid, calm, restful
<u>Persuasive</u> ...... convincing, believable, compelling, charming
<u>Perturbed</u> ...... uneasy, flustered, unsettled, flurried
<u>Pleasant</u> ...... satisfying, fulfilling, rewarding, gratifying
<u>Pleased</u> ...... thrilled, delighted, content, satisfied
<u>Poignant</u> ...... heartbreaking, distressing, moving, tear-jerking
<u>Poor</u> ...... destitute, indigent, penniless, impoverished
<u>Popular</u> ...... trendy, fashionable, admired, prevalent
<u>Positive</u> ...... optimistic, upbeat, affirmative, constructive
<u>Practical</u> ...... realistic, sensible, functional, doable, viable
<u>Presentable</u> ...... shipshape, well-groomed, tidy, personable
<u>Proper</u> ...... decorous, prim, orthodox, de rigueur, formulaic

Proud (1) ...... conceited, pompous, egotistical, smug
Proud (2) ...... appreciative, admiring, reverent, awed
Pure ...... unadulterated, wholesome, pristine, clean
Quiet ...... noiseless, silent, still, hushed, soundless
Rare ...... scarce, sparse, unique, exceptional, peerless
Realistic ...... genuine, credible, authentic, rational, true
Reasonable ...... equitable, judicious, sensible, practical, fair
Recent ...... the latest, current, fresh, up-to-date
Relevant ...... germane, pertinent, appropriate, significant
Relieved ...... worriless, reassured, comforted, calmed
Religious ...... spiritual, devout, pious, fervent, dedicated
Resilient ...... irrepressible, indestructible, durable, sturdy
Responsible ...... dependable, conscientious, reliable, steadfast
Rich ...... loaded, flush, affluent, moneyed, wealthy
Risky ...... perilous, hazardous, treacherous, precarious
Roomy ...... spacious, expansive, vast, palatial, commodious
Rough ...... coarse, jagged, rugged, craggy, gritty, broken
Rowdy ...... boisterous, disorderly, raucous, unruly, wild
Rude ...... vulgar, insolent, offensive, derogatory, boorish
Sad ...... desolate, disconsolate, wretched, dejected
Saddening ...... grieving, anguishing, discouraging, dispiriting
Safe ...... harmless, benign, secure, protected, sheltered
Same ...... identical, matching, indistinguishable, exact
Sassy ...... impertinent, cheeky, insolent, disrespectful
Scared ...... terrified, petrified, terror-stricken, panicked
Serious ...... solemn, somber, stern, dour, melancholy, grim
Severe ...... acute, grave, critical, serious, brutal, relentless
Sexy ...... seductive, steamy, provocative, erotic, sensual
Shaky ...... tremulous, quaking, vibrating, unsteady
Shiny ...... burnished, reflective, buffed, slick
Short ...... stubby, squat, dwarf, diminutive, petite
Shy ...... timid, backward, introverted, withdrawn
Significant ...... key, noteworthy, momentous, major, vital
Silky ...... sleek, smooth, satiny, glossy, lustrous, shiny
Similar ...... alike, akin, analogous, comparable, equivalent
Simple ...... easy, straightforward, effortless, uncomplicated
Slow ...... sluggish, sedate, plodding, creeping, snail-like
Small ...... tiny, miniscule, infinitesimal, microscopic, wee
Smart ...... canny, percipient, sapient, discerning, knowing
Smooth ...... flat, glassy, polished, level, even, unblemished
Soft ...... malleable, yielding, spongy, muted, doughy

Sorry ...... remorseful, repentant, penitent, contrite
Sour ...... acerbic, tart, vinegary, biting, harsh, caustic
Specific ...... precise, exact, explicit, definite, unambiguous
Spirited ...... feisty, animated, spunky, plucky, intrepid
Stinky ...... putrid, fetid, rank, rancid, putrescent, noxious
Straightforward ...... understandable, clear-cut, definitive, overt
Strange ...... weird, eerie, bizarre, uncanny, peculiar, odd
Strict ...... stern, austere, severe, rigorous, harsh, rigid
Strong ...... muscular, brawny, rugged, powerful, tough
Stubborn ...... unbending, immovable, intractable, obdurate
Stupid ...... idiotic, dense, vacuous, ridiculous, inane
Substantial ...... considerable, significant, extensive, ample
Successful ...... lucrative, productive, thriving, prosperous
Sudden ...... unexpected, abrupt, precipitous, unforeseen
Suitable ...... appropriate, fitting, seemly, proper, correct
Sure ...... positive, persuaded, certain, convinced
Suspicious ...... skeptical, distrustful, wary, guarded, leery
Sweet ...... syrupy, sugary, honeyed, cloying, treacly
Tactile ...... touchable, palpable, physical, perceptible
Tall ...... towering, lofty, multistory, soaring, statuesque
Tame ...... docile, submissive, meek, compliant, subdued
Tangled ...... matted, knotted, intertwined, entangled
Tasty ...... delectable, mouthwatering, scrumptious, divine
Tempting ...... irresistible, enticing, tantalizing, alluring
Tense ...... overwrought, rigid, taut, strained, agitated
Terrible ...... dreadful, horrendous, horrific, shocking
Thin ...... gaunt, scrawny, emaciated, haggard, skeletal
Tired ...... exhausted, spent, frazzled, bushed, drained
Traditional ...... conventional, established, customary, habitual
Treacherous ...... traitorous, disloyal, unfaithful, perfidious
Ugly ...... hideous, revolting, repugnant, grotesque
Unfair ...... unjust, bigoted, prejudiced, inequitable
Unlikely ...... improbable, implausible, doubtful, dubious
Unusual ...... abnormal, extraordinary, uncommon, unique
Upset ...... devastated, shook up, rattled, unglued
Urgent ...... life-and-death, earthshaking, pivotal, disastrous
Useful ...... expedient, effective, nifty, handy, valuable
Valuable ...... precious, priceless, treasured, inestimable
Violent ...... abusive, savage, barbarous, cutthroat, cruel
Visible ...... conspicuous, exposed, obvious, prominent
Voluptuous ...... buxom, curvaceous, chesty, busty, stacked

<u>Warm</u> ...... stifling, hot, sultry, sweltering, oppressive
<u>Wary</u> ...... skeptical, suspicious, leery, vigilant, distrustful
<u>Weak</u> ...... feeble, frail, delicate, debilitated, fragile, sickly
<u>Well</u> ...... superb, fine, fabulous, all right, okay, good
<u>Wet</u> ...... saturated, soaked, waterlogged, sopping
<u>Wicked</u> ...... evil, sinful, villainous, nefarious, fiendish
<u>Wide</u> ...... vast, expansive, sweeping, boundless, distended
<u>Widespread</u> ...... extensive, pervasive, prevalent, rampant
<u>Wild</u> ...... untamed, feral, unmanageable, uncontrollable
<u>Windy</u> ...... roaring, blustery, turbulent, howling, wild
<u>Wise</u> ...... sagacious, sage, astute, enlightened, shrewd
<u>Worn</u> ...... threadbare, shabby, frayed, tattered, ragged
<u>Worried</u> ...... distressed, distraught, overwrought, upset
<u>Young</u> ...... undeveloped, fledgling, immature, budding
<u>Zealous</u> ...... driven, ambitious, motivated, passionate

Went

How often do you rely on *went* when you send your protagonists somewhere?

Mike <u>went</u> to the office, and then Marlene <u>went</u> to the store.

Nothing in the preceding sentence provides any grasp of the situation.

What do we know about Mike and Marlene?

Is Mike happy about going to the office? Did he argue with Marlene before he left for work? Does he live within walking distance? Does he drive a car? Or perhaps ride a moped?

Consider the connotations of the following sentences:

Mike <u>rushed</u> to the office.

Mike <u>stormed</u> to the office.

Mike <u>plodded</u> to the office.

Mike <u>drove</u> to the office.

Mike <u>Segwayed</u> to the office.

Scrutinize Marlene. Is she irked because Mike used up all the milk without telling her? Did she win their argument? Is she forced to ride her bicycle because Mike took the car? So many verbs would be stronger than *went*:

Marlene <u>steamed</u> to the store.

Marlene <u>stomped</u> to the store.

Marlene <u>breezed</u> to the store.

Marlene <u>chugged</u> to the store.

Marlene <u>biked</u> to the store.

Search through your work in progress to locate all occurrences of the verb *to go*. Replace with stronger verbs from the list. If a word is close but not quite right, consult your favorite thesaurus for an alternative.

Watch for all the forms of *to go*.

go
goes
went
am going
is going
have gone
has gone
will go
will have gone
was going
were going
had gone
will be going
have been going
has been going
had been going
will have been going
having gone

You might be surprised to see how often you depend on this verb in its various tenses.

Alternatives for *went*:

<u>A</u>
Absconded, accompanied, advanced, ambled, ambulated, ankled, approached, arrowed, ascended

<u>B</u>
Bailed, banked, barged, barreled, beat it, beelined, biked, blasted off, blazed, blew by, blundered, bolted, boogied, booted, bounced, bounded, breezed, broke, brushed, budged, bugged out, bulled past, burst, bustled

C

Cantered, capered, careened, careered, caromed, cast off, cavorted, charged, chuffed, chugged, circled, clambered, cleared out, climbed, clomped, clopped, clumped, clunked, coasted, coursed, crashed, crawled, crept, crossed, cruised, curved, cut and run, cut through, cycled

D

Danced, darted, dashed, dawdled, decamped, defected, departed, descended, disappeared, dislocated, disturbed, dived/dove, doddered, dogged it, dragged, drifted, dropped, drove, ducked out

E

Eased, edged, elbowed through, eluded, emigrated, encroached, entered, escaped, escorted, evacuated, evaded, evaporated, excursed, exited

F

Faded, fell, filed, flapped, fled, flew, flitted, flittered, floated, flopped, flounced, floundered, flowed, fluttered, followed, footed it, forged, frolicked

G

Gadded, gallivanted, galloped, galumphed, gamboled, gimped, glided, glissaded, goose-stepped, ground

H

Hastened, headed for, hied, hightailed, hiked, hit the road, hitched forward, hobbled, hoofed it, hopped, hotfooted it, humped, hurdled, hurried, hurtled, hustled

I

Impelled, inched, itinerated

J

Jerked, jetted, jogged, journeyed, jumped

K

Knocked about

L
Launched, led, lead-footed it, leaped/leapt, left, legged it, lighted out/lit out, limped, locomoted, loitered, loped, lumbered, lunged, lurched

M
Made a break, made haste, made off, made tracks, marched, maundered, meandered, migrated, minced, moped, moseyed, motored, mounted, moved, moved out, muscled

N
Navigated, neared, negotiated, nosed, nose-dived

O
Offloaded

P
Paced, padded, paddled, paraded, passed, patrolled, peeled, pelted off, penetrated, perambulated, peregrinated, pirouetted, pitter-pattered, plodded, plowed, plummeted, plunged, positioned, pottered, pounced, pranced, proceeded, progressed, promenaded, propelled, prowled, pulled out, pushed ahead, pushed away, pushed off, pushed on, puttered

Q
Quit/quitted

R
Raced, rambled, rammed, ran, ranged, rattled, rebounded, receded, recoiled, reeled, relocated, removed, repaired, resettled, retired, retreated, retrogressed, returned, ricocheted, roamed, rocketed, rode, rolled, romped, rose, roved, rowed, rumbled, rushed

S
Sailed, sallied forth, sashayed, sauntered, scaled, scampered, scattered, scooted, scrabbled, scrambled, scrammed, scudded, scuffed, scurried, scuttled, Segwayed, serpentined, set off, shambled, shifted, shimmied, shipped, shot, shouldered through, shoved off, shrank, shuffled, sidestepped, skateboarded, skated, skedaddled, skidded, skied, skipped, skipped out, skirred, skirted, skittered, skulked, skyrocketed, sledded, slid, slipped, slithered, slogged, slunk,

smoked, snaked, snuck, soared, sped, spiraled, split, sprang, sprinted, spurted, staggered, stalked, stamped, stampeded, steamed, steered, stepped, stirred, stole away, stomped, stormed, straggled, strayed, streaked, streamed, strode, strolled, struck out, strutted, stumbled, stumped, swaggered, swam, swayed, swept, swished away, switched, swooshed

T
Tailed, threaded, thundered, tiptoed, toddled, took off, tore, tottered, toured, trailed, traipsed, tramped, trampled, transferred, transported, transposed, traveled, traversed, trekked, tripped, trod, tromped, trooped, trotted, trudged, tumbled, twirled

V
Vacated, vamoosed, vanished, vaulted, veered, ventured

W
Waddled, waded, wafted, walked, waltzed, wandered, weaved, wended, wheeled, whipped, whisked, whizzed, whooshed, wiggled, winged, withdrew, wobbled, wormed, wove, wriggled

Z
Zipped, zoomed

Overused Punctuation

Are you a punctuation junkie?

Exclamation points.

Ellipses.

Em dashes.

They provide clarity when used well but annoy readers if overexploited.

This section will help you conquer your overdependence on *!*, ..., and —.

Ellipses ... Bane or Blessing?

Before we begin, let's consider the definition of *ellipsis:*

"a sign (such as ...) used in printed text to show that words have been left out."

An ellipsis can also indicate a pause, or an unfinished thought or sentence. Scattered judiciously, ellipses add clarity and character to a piece.

Creative writers most commonly lean on ellipses to show pauses in speech or action. Depending on the style guide, you'll see either of two approaches:

She stopped at the door ... and waited.

She stopped at the door . . . and waited.

Both are complete sentences that could also be expressed as:

She stopped at the door and waited.

Consider the differences between the preceding examples and these.

She stopped at the door. ... It was locked.

She stopped at the door. . . . It was locked.

A pause in action separates two complete sentences. The first sentence ends with a period, which is followed by a space, an ellipsis, and another complete sentence.

Note: There is no such thing as a four-dot ellipsis. I repeat, and the style guides agree: <u>There is no such thing as a four-dot ellipsis</u>.

Consider the following examples.

The teacher spoke so rapidly that the student was unable to record everything she said. "The world is dying. ... floods, earthquakes. We must act now."

The teacher spoke so rapidly that the student was unable to record everything she said. "The world is dying. . . . floods, earthquakes. We must act now."

The second example seems to contain a four-dot ellipsis. However, the four dots represent the closing period of a complete sentence, a space, and a three-dot ellipsis to indicate a missing word or words, plus the rest of the quoted speech.

Spaces ... spaces. Don't omit the spaces.

Style guides agree on one point:

All ellipses should be set off by spaces.

Correct:

She stopped at the door ... and waited.

She stopped at the door . . . and waited.

Incorrect:

She stopped at the door...and waited.

She stopped at the door. . .and waited.

If you omit the surrounding spaces, this is how your words could split at the end of a sentence:

Julie heard something in the hall. She stopped at the door...and waited.

Julie heard something in the hall. She stopped at the door. . .and waited.

Software treats the combination of *door...and* as a single word. When you use spaces as the style guides recommend, sentence splits appear more logical. You might see something like:

Julie heard something in the hall. She stopped at the door ... and waited.

Because ellipses are *sticky* punctuation, they remain attached to the words they adjoin.

The only time you break the rule about surrounding ellipses with spaces is in this type of situation:

She yelled, "Get out or ..."

She yelled, "Get out or . . ."

If you precede the closing quotation mark with a space, you could end up with the following scenario, isolating the quotation mark at the beginning of an empty line:

She yelled, "Get out or ...
"

She yelled, "Get out or . . .
"

Why I don't like . . . ellipses.

If you use the . . . approach, Microsoft Word and many other text editors will count each period as a separate word. When you're writing flash fiction or short stories where economy of words is important, that can create a huge problem.

This sentence counts as five words in MS-Word: *He whirled ... and fell.*

This one as seven: *He whirled . . . and fell.*

Another difficulty with . . . ellipses is the way they often divide at the end of a line. You could wind up with confusing splits like:

She stopped at the door . .
. and waited.

That's unattractive and confusing.

Non-breaking spaces between the dots solve the problem, but not all software makes it easy to insert them. The key sequence in MS Word for a non-breaking space is CTRL-SHIFT-SPACE.

To convert the ellipsis in *He whirled . . . and fell*, the MS-Word sequence would be:

He whirled [SPACE] . [CTRL-SHIFT-SPACE] . [CTRL-SHIFT-SPACE] . [SPACE] *and fell.*

Why ... why ... *why?*

We live in the twenty-first century. Why do some style guides, publishers, and copyeditors still cling to the old-fashioned dot-space-dot-space-dot ellipsis?

It's ugly. It's word-bloating.

Let's kick it to the curb.

Should you belong to *Ellipses Anonymous*?

You know who you are.

An ellipsis here ... an ellipsis there ... and soon you have a WIP scattered with so many dots it looks like a petri dish overflowing with exotic bacteria.

Consider the following.

"Er ... um ... ," said Alyssa. "I ... uh ... think I ... love you, Leon."

Please. Kill. Me. Now.

The narrator wants to show Alyssa's hesitation, but the excessive ellipses will annoy readers.

Better:

Alyssa stared at the floor, scuffing the carpet with one toe. A blush blossomed in her cheeks. "I think I love you, Leon."

A second example:

A cat in heat yowled somewhere ... nearby. Andrew reached into his pocket for his revolver ...

The first ellipsis demonstrates that Andrew isn't quite sure where the cat is. The second shows a trailing off to indicate that something happens, or that there is a lapse in time, but it doesn't give readers any details.

Better:

A cat in heat yowled somewhere nearby. Andrew reached into his pocket for his revolver. He turned to face whoever was shuffling behind him.

A third example:

"But you know there are other reasons ..." Jill bit her lip.

If readers know the reasons, an ellipsis is extraneous. If they aren't aware of the reasons, why not list them?

Better:

"But Bill is busy, the dog bites strangers, and I can't afford a dog sitter." Jill bit her lip.

Now readers don't have to guess the backstory.

A fourth example:

Akela searched ... and ... paced ... and searched again. The ring was nowhere to be found.

Try this instead:

Akela searched. She paced. She searched again. No ring.

In moments of tension, short sentences work best.

A fifth example:

Apples ... oranges ... bananas ... pears ... spilled from the cart, making the street look more like a fruit salad than a thoroughfare.

Why the ellipses? Commas would work just as well.

Apples, oranges, bananas, and pears spilled from the cart, making the street look more like a fruit salad than a thoroughfare.

Search through your WIP.

Analyze every ellipsis. Would your writing be stronger without it? Overused ellipses are just as annoying as overdone words, perhaps more so.

An exercise in conciseness and creativity.

Remove all ellipses in the following to create micro fiction, or build on the examples and milk them as story prompts for longer pieces.

1. "I don't care ... it's just ... I can't." Brandy ran her fingers through her hair ... so thin ... so brittle. "No more treatments ... no more ... I've had enough."

2. Brit skulked forward on all fours ... One palm squished into something warm ... squishy. "Crap," she muttered.

Hayley suppressed a giggle ... and whispered, "I told you it was a bad idea ... you know ... to rob this place right after the dog walker came through."

3. The moon rose ... huge over a rugged skyline with jutting trees ... ragged rocks ... a flat plateau to the right ... An owl's hoot pierced the sharp night air ... filling it with an eerie quality ... a sound that slithered up Susan's spine like a serpent.

Em Dash Abuse—It Ain't Pretty

Abuse—overuse—misuse—whatever you call it—too much is too much.

How often do you insert em dashes in your writing—and why? ... Although occasional em dashes can clarify—or emphasize—phrases—and clauses—their appearance can annoy readers—and editors. Misuse transforms them into obnoxious interruptions—especially when combined with ellipsis overuse. Too-frequent reliance on these punctuation marks—just like overworked words—will grate nerves ... and make your writing appear akin to an alien language rather than prose—as illustrated by this annoying—and poorly written—paragraph. ...

What are em dashes, and why would you need them?

An em dash is a long dash that takes up approximately the same amount of horizontal space as the letter *M*. To form an em dash, type two hyphens. You can configure word processors such as Word to convert the hyphens into em dashes. The INSERT SYMBOL function offers another way to access them.

Writers exploit em dashes as replacements for or indicators of:

- Commas
- Semicolons
- Colons
- Parentheses
- Emphasis
- Interruptions
- Sudden breaks
- Trailing off

Style guides offer two methods for adjacent spacing.

According to *The Chicago Manual of Style*, you should not separate em dashes with spaces. *The Associated Press Stylebook* states the opposite.

The Chicago Manual of Style approach:

Never use peanut butter—or almond paste—in this recipe.

The Associated Press Stylebook approach:

Never use peanut butter — or almond paste — in this recipe.

Em dashes, like ellipses, are *sticky* punctuation. They stay attached to words if not set off by spaces.

Following the *Chicago Manual of Style* recommendation, you could end up with a split like this at the end of a line:

The man tipped his hat and said,
"Supercalifragilisticexpialidocious—that's wot I always says to chaps
on the street."

The same sentence written according to *The Associated Press Stylebook* guidelines would divide better:

The man tipped his hat and said, "Supercalifragilisticexpialidocious —
that's wot I always says to chaps on the street."

Note: the shorter the words around the em dash, the less likely you will be to encounter spacing difficulties.

Try something like this instead of the preceding examples:

The man tipped his hat and said, "G'day—that's wot I always says to
chaps on the street."

Better yet:

The man tipped his hat and said, "G'day's wot I always says to chaps on
the street."

No em dash at all will usually yield the best visual experience.

Interrupted dialogue poses spacing problems too.

No matter which style guide you follow, an em dash preceding a quotation mark could result in a break that leaves a closing quotation mark at the beginning of a new line:

"I never wanted to go in—
"

Although workarounds like non-breaking thin spaces might solve the problem, they cause unpredictable results in some platforms used by self-publishers.

Beware quotation marks that face the wrong way.

Do you see something like this whenever you end dialogue with an em dash?

"I never wanted to go in—"

Note the closing quote mark. To fix this in Microsoft Word, type the following key sequence for the end of the sentence:

i n ″ [CURSOR BACK] - -

In other words, you resolve the problem by typing the quotation mark first and then cursoring back to insert the em dash.

Evaluate your options.

Perform a final search before submitting or publishing, and analyze every em dash.

- Would a comma or semicolon function better?

- A colon?

- Parentheses?

- A new sentence or paragraph?

- Perhaps a change in word order would solve the problem.

Consider these examples.

She does the cooking—and I always clean up the mess.

The words around the em dash are short. Good. However, a semicolon would function just as well.

She does the cooking; and I always clean up the mess.

Are you a semicolon hater? Try a comma instead.

She does the cooking, and I always clean up the mess.

If you don't mind starting a sentence with *and*, the next edit would also make the point. Perhaps with better effect.

She does the cooking. And I always clean up the mess.

A second example:

Professor Tomkins insists on three things—prompt attendance at all lectures, no cell phones, and no holey blue jeans.

Since the words before the em dash introduce a list, a colon would provide an appropriate alternative.

Professor Tomkins insists on three things: prompt attendance at all lectures, no cell phones, and no holey blue jeans.

Or you could reorganize the sentence.

Professor Tomkins insists that everyone arrive at his lectures on time, and he has banned cell phones and holey blue jeans.

A third example:

Brandie's agent—Karen Arthurs—requests an upfront deposit.

Commas would do a more effective job.

Brandie's agent, Karen Arthurs, requests an upfront deposit.

Fourth example:

While jogging his regular route—over seven miles of hilly terrain—Wayne listened to classical music.

Parentheses could replace the em dashes.

While jogging his regular route (over seven miles of hilly terrain) Wayne listened to classical music.

Disclaimer: Many editors dislike parentheses in fiction, preferring commas or alternative punctuation.

While jogging his regular route, over seven miles of hilly terrain, Wayne listened to classical music.

You could make a strong case for removing the first comma.

While jogging his regular route over seven miles of hilly terrain, Wayne listened to classical music.

Final example:

"I always wanted a backpack like this," Tori tugged at the packaging, "—and I can't wait to show it to Lucius."

The punctuation is correct. However, there's no need for an em dash.

"I always wanted a backpack like this," Tori tugged at the packaging, "and I can't wait to show it to Lucius."

Because the action beat interrupts dialogue, you capitalize and punctuate it as though it were a dialogue tag. If that makes you nervous, try rewording.

Tori tugged at the packaging. "I always wanted a backpack like this, and I can't wait to show it to Lucius."

Or:

"I always wanted a backpack like this," Tori said as she tugged at the packaging, "and I can't wait to show it to Lucius."

Sometimes you shouldn't eliminate em dashes.

Consider this sentence.

Many chefs say this is the best way—no, the only way—to cook perfect rice.

If you were to replace the em dashes with commas, you would end up with the following.

Many chefs say this is the best way, no, the only way, to cook perfect rice.

The series of commas could confuse readers. Therefore, in this instance, em dashes function best.

As always, let your writing rest between edits. When you review your work with new perspective, awkward constructions will reveal themselves, especially when you read your words out loud.

Ready to test your creativity? Try these exercises and story prompts.

Edit to remove all or most em dashes.

1. "I must admit—" Captain Corliss stopped talking to his second-in-command—hand extended toward the airlock. A shape shimmered—between him and his escape route—sending a shiver creeping up his spine. "Who are you?" he demanded, "—and what is a Zanomorph doing on my ship?"

[Why are the captain and his second-in-command trying to leave their ship? Are they attempting an escape? What is a Zanomorph?]

2. Nobody could tell—any more than I—why people avoided looking into my eyes. Some days I spent minutes—or hours—gazing at my reflection in the mirror. I didn't look so different—and I didn't think I felt any different—than my coworkers—my family—my friends. I had two eyes—two ears—a bright smile. Women said I was handsome—whenever they stole a quick glance.

I tried over a dozen brands of deodorant—umpteen kinds of toothpaste—and even dyed my hair.

Nothing worked.

I felt isolated—alone—unloved. Only one solution remained. Did I dare try it?

[Does the narrator suffer from a mental condition? Perhaps he's an alien or a fantasy being. Invent a solution that matches the narrator's identity.]

3. Two more miles—just two more miles—until I reached Seraphina. I couldn't wait to gaze into her gorgeous eyes—taste her sweet lips—squeeze her until she squealed. My breaths heaved in ever-shorter gasps—each one forcing a stab of pain into my chest. I tripped over something—a root perhaps—and stumbled.

As I plummeted—in slow motion—toward the forest floor—a cackle sounded from behind me. "It ain't that easy, sonny boy—you still have three more challenges—before you scale the mountain and mount the lovely maiden."

[Seraphina means *fiery ones*. The Seraphim of the Bible are angels with six wings. Could that play a part in your story?]

4. "Unsurpassed verbiage—and unparalleled parallels," murmured the professor—as he stroked his white beard. "Excellent—excellent—I will read your story to the class, Ms.—uh—Ms. ..."

Mitra's eyes flashed with fury. "Ms. Melek."

"Yes—yes—yes. Ms. Mallard." He tapped at his hearing aid—and he blushed—a red rivalling that of a ripe tomato. "Uh—and why are you here—Ms.—uh—Ms. ...?"

"You summoned me here—for an interview—as your assistant—sir." She extended her hand.

The professor blinked. "Ah—I—" He reached across his desk and shook her hand. "Nice to meet you—Ms. ..." His eyes lost focus—he slumped in his chair—and slid to the floor.

[Who is Mitra? A student? An assassin? Did she administer something to the professor via the handshake? Is he suffering from dementia? Has somebody already poisoned him?]

Exclamation Points! Plague or Pleasure?

Let's review what a few famous writers have said about exclamation points.

"Cut out all these exclamation points. An exclamation point is like laughing at your own joke." ~ F. Scott Fitzgerald

"But the teller of the comic story does not slur the nub; he shouts it at you—every time. And when he prints it, in England, France, Germany, and Italy, he italicizes it, puts some whooping exclamation-points after it, and sometimes explains it in a parenthesis. All of which is very depressing, and makes one want to renounce joking and lead a better life." ~ Mark Twain

"Keep your exclamation points under control. You are allowed no more than two or three per 100,000 words of prose." ~ Elmore Leonard

To summarize, F. Scott Fitzgerald hated exclamation points; Mark Twain didn't like them either; Elmore Leonard recommended only two or three per novel.

Do you agree?

Merriam-Webster defines an exclamation point as "a mark *!* used especially after an interjection or exclamation to indicate forceful utterance or strong feeling."

Let's compare exclamation points to a fine glass of wine. One glass glides over the tongue, exciting the taste buds. The second glass lacks the same appeal, and it dulls the senses. Each succeeding glass decreases awareness, until you finally pass out.

Can you imagine the following?

Ward stopped in the hallway outside his apartment. Did he hear someone inside? His pulse raced. He unlocked the door and creaked it open a crack.

With trembling fingers, he groped for the light switch.

"Surprise," said a chorus of voices.

The preceding example contains no exclamation points and adheres to the rule of never using anything except *said* to attribute dialogue. *Surprise* comes across as deadpan. Lifeless.

Let's loosen the rules straitjacket.

"Surprise!" yelled a chorus of voices.

Now we see a forceful utterance, as per the preceding dictionary definition.

I could have written another version.

"Surprise!!!!!" screeched a cacophonous chorus of voices."

Does the overstatement make the sentence stronger?

No.

Multiple exclamation points dilute rather than augment. As Terry Pratchett said, five exclamation marks are "the sure sign of an insane mind." *Screeched* is too much of a departure from *said*, and *cacophonous* transforms the excerpt into a prime example of purple prose.

As with any punctuation, exclamation points have a place. Your task is to make them complement your writing without irritating readers.

Situations where you might use an exclamation point:

- A character is in extreme danger.

- An exciting or horrific situation unfolds.

- A person shouts, protests, or interjects.

- Someone issues a strong command.

As an aside, German requires an exclamation point in imperative mood. Although English stemmed from Germanic roots, this convention no longer applies.

Nobody wants a novel that reads like a comic strip.

Generous sprinkling of exclamation points, although suitable for comics or children's books, will irritate adults.

Consider a few examples.

Bill punched the wall with one fist. Bash! "If I've told you once, I've told you a million times, don't put cinnamon in my coffee!!!!!"

Bill's punch and dialogue show his anger.

Bill bashed the wall with one fist. "If I've told you once, I've told you a million times, don't put cinnamon in my coffee."

Punched is changed to *bashed*. Zero exclamation points. F. Scott Fitzgerald would approve, although you might prefer a single *!* at the end of the paragraph.

Todd said, "She has to say yes! She just has to! I don't know what I'll do if she turns me down!"

We see a desperate Todd. Do the exclamation points help?

Not really.

Todd said, "She has to say yes. She has to. I don't know what I'll do if she turns me down."

The preceding version eliminates *just* and all three exclamation points, but it lacks emotion. Would it be better with appropriate body language?

Todd trembled. "She has to say yes. She has to. I don't know what I'll do if she turns me down."

Todd's trembling shows his anguish. Note that the dialogue tag becomes an action beat when changed to *Todd trembled*.

"No!" yelled Grandma. "You're not allowed outside until you clean your room!"

Unless we're reading a confrontational scene, Grandma seems overwrought or maybe even mean.

"No," said Grandma, "you're not allowed outside until you clean your room."

Now we see a calm situation. However, if Grandma is annoyed, let's make it obvious.

"No," said Grandma as she waggled her finger, "you're not allowed outside until you clean your room."

The waggling finger shows Grandma's annoyance. But maybe she's furious.

Grandma's eyes flashed. She leaned forward and poked Johnny's chest. "No. You're not allowed outside until you clean your room."

Subtle changes open different emotional curtains. Making *No* a separate sentence adds emphasis without *!* to make the point.

"You've got to be kidding!!!" Sam said. "I'd never do that!"

Try this instead:

"You've got to be kidding," Sam said. "I'd. Never. Do. That."

The lowly period provides emphasis, and exclamation points are reserved for those situations where readers will notice them.

Have you ever seen something like this?

"What the?!" Trent exclaimed. "Nobody gave you permission to take that apple pie."

Is Trent asking a question or expressing an emotion such as anger? Let's make it clear.

"What the—" Trent glared and pointed to the apple pie on my plate. "Nobody gave you permission to take that."

No exclamation point or question mark, and we replace the dialogue tag with an action beat that shows Trent's anger.

"What the—" Trent raised his eyebrows and pointed to the apple pie on my plate. "Did somebody give you permission to take that?"

Now we see a clear indication of uncertainty with Trent's raised eyebrows and the question mark.

Text messages require special treatment.

Fitzgerald, Leonard, and Twain might have altered their advice if they had lived long enough to experience the texting revolution. Although serious writing should shun multiple exclamation points, texting provides an entertaining exception to the rule.

Kim: OMG. U should be here.

Cal: Why?

Kim: I just saw Lady Gaga.

Cal: OMW

Writing should mirror life. Can you imagine anyone texting the above without exclamation points?

Better:

Kim: OMG!!!!!! U should be here!

Cal: Why?

Kim: I just saw Lady Gaga!!!!

Cal: OMW!!!!!

Or the senders might tap out texts like this:

Kim: Omg u shud be here

Cal: Why

Kim: I just saw lady gaga

Cal: On my way!

In moments of fast communication, people omit punctuation and capitalization, allowing their phones to replace expressions like *Omw* with *On my way!*

If in doubt about texts in a story, send a series of messages to yourself and note the changes in format. When in a hurry, you're less likely to insert emoticons, punctuation, or symbols.

Some types of writing demand strict adherence to the *no exclamation point* rule.

Exclamation points have no place in:

- Résumés

- Financial reports

- Business correspondence

- Book reports

- College essays

A well-placed *!* will call attention to a statement. However, if you want to project a professional image, words do it better. Review the following extract from an interdepartmental memo.

Thanks for sending the budget proposal! It will be very helpful at the next staff meeting!

This might be a communication between associates, or a boss and one of the employees. Exclamation points, although accepted by many in this type of environment, broadcast unprofessionalism.

I can't thank you enough for sending the budget proposal. It will be indispensable at the next staff meeting.

The words *show* gratitude. A change from *very helpful* to *indispensable* tightens the writing.

Ready to tackle a few exercises and story prompts?

Edit the following, removing all or most exclamation points. Grab them as story prompts if you wish.

1. "Nobody can do a better job of training your dog than me!" exclaimed Hans. "Heck, I've been at this for nigh on twenty years now!!!"

"If you're so good," exclaimed Helga, "why is your dog peeing on your pant leg?!"

2. Lightning flashed! Thunder boomed! A crack like a gunshot rang out as the old maple tree toppled onto the street.

"No!" I cried. "No! No! No!" My stash of [Jewels? Coke? Something funny he doesn't want his wife to know about?] spilled out of the hollow trunk.

3. "No seasickness on a cruise?! BS!!!!" I hung over the rail and barfed up my breakfast!

Sandy slapped my face! And then she shoved me! Me, her husband of twenty-six years!

Time stood still as I plummeted toward the giant waves. Salty spray licked at my face.

Suddenly, I saw a dark shape churning the water below me.

Shark! No, many sharks!!! [Does our protagonist really see sharks, or is something else lurking in the water? Do you kill him off and then use flashbacks to show how he got to this point? Or is this the beginning of an adventure? Perhaps he is whisked away to another time or dimension. Is *suddenly* necessary?]

4. Emma sang as she skipped over the sidewalk. "Step on a crack; break your mother's back! Step ..." Something wet and squishy pelted her back.

She stopped. Her freckled face contorted into a crooked frown. "Frankie, stop that!"

Frankie darted out from behind a hedge several feet in front of her. "Stop what?" His eyes widened! He pointed to something behind her!

Emma whirled around! [Does she see something scary? Funny? Would this work as an opener for a children's book or short story?]

Taboos

When Milton coined the phrase "Every cloud has a silver lining" in *Comus*, readers loved it.

However, nowadays it's considered cliché, and your editor will likely strike it out.

Other no-no's include overstatement and overreliance on cursing.

The following chapters cover a few common writing taboos.

Absolute Adjectives

Absolute adjectives, also called non-gradable adjectives, embody a quality that is 100 percent in degree. Can a person be more than 100 percent alive? Less? More than 100 percent pregnant?

By definition, absolutes shouldn't be modified by qualifiers. That includes adverbs *very, really, approximately, rather, quite, almost,* and their cousins.

Prefixes provide clues.

an: not, without
anti: against
de: opposite
dis: not, opposite of
ever: always, continuously
il, im, in, ir: not
mis: wrongly
non: not
omni: all
over: over, too much
pre: before
super: above, beyond
un: not, opposite of
under: under, too little
whole: completely, all

Exercise caution whenever you see adjectives that start with the foregoing prefixes.

Anhydrous: containing no water
Can a substance contain *approximately no water? Very no water?*

Anti-abortion: opposing or against abortion
A person can be *anti-abortion* or *pro-abortion*. You might describe someone as *rabidly anti-abortion* to show zeal, but *very anti-abortion* is weak writing. People are *pro-* or *anti-*, but not *very pro-* or *extremely anti-* anything.

Nonfat: containing no fat
Could you ever describe a dish as *really nonfat? Rather nonfat?* A food contains fat or it doesn't. Period.

Uncolored: having no color; colorless
If something has the slightest tinge of color, you can't refer to it as *uncolored.* You might describe it as *barely pink* or *off-white,* but never *quite uncolored.*

Overjoyed: filled with great joy
Can someone be any more joyful than *overjoyed?* Can a stove be more heated than *overheated?* Can a lesson be more simple than *oversimplified?*

Suffixes also indicate absolutes.

able, ible: capable of being
est: the most
free: free of, free from
ful: full of
less: without
worthy: deserving of, fit for

If a planet is *airless,* can it have any air? If tea is *caffeine-free,* can it be described as *fairly caffeine-free?* Can a *wonderful* writer be *more wonderful* than a colleague?

Pay attention to colors.

Black is black and white is white. Astute writers avoid phrases such as *really black* and *very white.* You're creative enough to invent something different, aren't you?

Which do you prefer?

Brandon's very black eyes filled me with fear.

Brandon's eyes glowed as black as his traitorous heart, overwhelming me with fear.

The second example bestows a degree of blackness to Brandon's eyes by comparing them to his personality. Although *traitorous heart* is a *tell*, you might need several paragraphs to describe why the narrator thinks Brandon is a traitor. Instead, you could use the description as foreshadowing or transition into backstory.

Serena's dress was so white and tight that it turned the head of every man in the room.

Serena's dress hugged her curves, a frosty web of white singing a siren song to every man in the room.

A frosty web of white presents a vivid image. Much better than *so white*, don't you think?

Colors are vibrant. They tinge, saturate, and radiate. *Deep red* is weak. Alternatives could be *black-cherry red, wound red,* or *beet red.*

If you have a Pinterest account, try searching for your target color with a phrase such as "things that are [INSERT COLOR]."

Speaking of Pinterest, please pay me a visit. You'll find me at

Pinterest.com/KathySteinemann

Absolute adjectives shouldn't be mixed with comparative and superlative.

You can't have a *completer, more complete,* or *completest/most complete* result. There is no such thing as a *wronger, more wrong,* or *wrongest/most wrong* opinion.

A lover might tell a woman she's the "most perfect beauty on Earth," but a writer shouldn't describe her that way except in dialogue.

Never use *more* with the comparative or *most* with the superlative. Avoid phrases like *more obscurer* and *most obscurest,* even in dialogue, unless your character is woefully uneducated.

Watch for the following words.

Scrutinize your writing. Although you might wish to modify these adjectives, they usually function better on their own.

Unless your intent is to make a point with sarcasm or irony, consider the examples in this list absolutes, and don't precede them with adverbs of degree.

A
Absent, absolute, abusive, accurate, active, acute, adequate, adjacent, adjoining, alert, alive, ample, ancient, animated, apparent, asleep, authorized, autonomous, avoidable, awake, aware, awash, away

B
Basic, beaten, best, bilateral, black, blameless, blank, boiling, bottommost, boundless, breathtaking, brimming, broken

C
Central, certain, chief, cognizant, collective, committed, common, communal, comparable, complete, concise, conclusive, condensed, confirmed, conscious, contiguous, conventional, correct, critical, crucial, crushed, cubical

D
Dead, decimated, defeated, defective, deficient, definite, destroyed, devastated, devoid, different, dire, discarnate, dispensable, domestic, drenched, duplicate

E
Effective, empty, enough, entire, equal, equitable, equivalent, essential, established, eternal, everyday, everything, evident, exact, exhilarated, expendable, extensive, extinct, extraordinary

F
Faithful, faithless, fake, false, fatal, faulty, figuratively, final, finest, finite, first, fixed, flat, flawless, foreign, foremost, foreseeable, freezing, frequent, full, functional, fundamental

G
Gone, grave, greatest, guiltless, guilty

H
Halfway, harmless, hopeful, hopeless

I

Ideal, identical, immediate, imminent, immortal, impartial, imperfect, impossible, improper, inaccurate, inactive, inadequate, incommunicado, incomparable, incomplete, inconsistent, incorrect, incorrigible, incurable, independent, indispensable, individual, inert, inevitable, inexact, inferior, infinite, informed, ingrained, innermost, innocent, insincere, insufficient, intact, intangible, intelligible, intentional, intoxicated, invalid, invulnerable, irrefutable, irregular, irrevocable

J

Joint, justifiable

K

Key, known

L

Lacking, last, left, lighted, lightless, limitless, literally, local, lowermost

M

Main, major, malfunctioning, manifest, married, matching, matchless, maximal, meaningful, meaningless, melting, merciless, middle, midway, mindful, minimal, minor, missing, mortal, multiple, mutual

N

Necessary, needless, nethermost, nuclear

O

Obscure, obvious, occupied, off, omnipotent, omnipresent, on, opaque, operational, opposite, outermost, outright, overall, overflowing, overheated, overjoyed, overstocked, overwhelmed

P

Packed, paramount, partial, passable, penultimate, perfect, perpetual, pivotal, popular, possible, powerless, precise, predominant, preeminent, preferable, pregnant, premeditated, present, preventable, primary, primitive, principal, private, proximate, public, pure

R

Rare, real, redundant, replete, requited, revocable, right, round, rudimentary, ruined, ruthless

S

Sacrosanct, safe, same, satisfactory, saturated, secondary, sentient, set, shattered, sheer, sighted, silent, sincere, single, singular, smashed, soaked, solitary, sopping, spotless, square, starving, stationary, staunch, stereotypical, straight, straightforward, stunning, successful, sufficient, suitable, superfluous, superior, superlative, supreme, sure, surplus, swarming

T

Tacit, tangible, teeming, temporary, tertiary, thorough, topmost, total, transparent, true

U

Ultimate, unanimous, unavoidable, unblemished, unbounded, unbroken, unclear, unclouded, unconditional, undecided, unequal, unequivocal, unforeseeable, uniform, unilateral, unimportant, uninformed, unique, universal, unknown, unlimited, unmarried, unnecessary, unpopular, unprecedented, unqualified, unquestionable, unrequited, unsafe, unsighted, unspoken, unsuccessful, up, utter

V

Vacant, valid, valuable, valueless, vapid, vital, vocal, void, vulnerable

W

Waterlogged, weighted, weightless, white, whole, widespread, willful, worst, wrecked, wrong

Cursing

The truth is ...

It's unrealistic to expect that a novel about truckers or construction workers would have them yelling "golly gee" or "shucks" when they're angry. Cursing is an inescapable part of life. A well-placed cuss can relieve tension, express annoyance, or tune in an adversary.

Careful. You lose fans if you overdo.

Some readers are intimidated by even a single word of profanity. Your writing will appeal to a larger audience if you exercise the same care avoiding cursing that you do avoiding unnecessary adverbs.

But zero profanity is often unrealistic.

So how can you make your writing lifelike without resorting to F-bombs or other expletives? You, the author, are a tightrope walker tiptoeing a shaky wire between reality and comedy.

Yes, comedy.

If you overdo the cursing, your work will come off like the amusing tirade of an angry adolescent. Eliminate all but the occasional necessary swear word.

Swearing in made-up worlds is easy.

Think of the most despicable character or beast in your created world. Your villain could be described as a *son of a [insert character or beast]*. Or, if your world is ruled by women, you might change *son* to *daughter*.

Other possibilities could include *spawn of a space sow*, *brood of a black star*, or *progeny of a wormhole*.

If your fictional world is an alternate Earth, you could use terms such as *son of a snake*, *son of a cur*, or *daughter of a slug*.

Battlestar Galactica invented *frak* and *felgercarb*.

Firefly used *gorram.*

Other movies or series came out with words such as *frell, poodoo, dren, Mik'ta, shazbot, drokk,* and *frag.*

Profanity in "real-world" fiction can be just as simple.

To continue with the *son of/daughter of* expressions, stories based in the past might use *son of a gun* or *daughter of the devil.*

Scrutinize the following sentences for alternative ways to portray cursing.

- An explosion of expletives turned the air blue.

- Antiquated obscenities sprang from his lips.

- She filled the air with ripe invective.

- She spouted graphic one-syllable words of derision.

- He swore fluently.

- He flooded the office with articulate curses.

- He mouthed a feral blasphemy.

- Effusive imprecations flooded the room.

- A chorus of four-letter words exploded from her lips.

- She uttered a litany of curses too foul to repeat.

- Ripe speech was his specialty. He used it now. In spades.

- Her stream of cussing superfluities burned my ears.

- He spewed an entire dictionary of crude sailor's words.

- His stevedore mouth exploded all over the bystanders.

Norman Mailer used *fug* in *The Naked and the Dead.* Was he any smarter or more innovative than you?

Dialogue can make the point without cursing.

"Shut the front door!"

"If I wanted your opinion, I'd have asked for it."

"Who do you think you're kidding?"

"Get out of here before I kill you."

"You gotta be jokin'!"

"You're more despicable than a meal-time telemarketer."

"My last deposit in the toilet had more character than you."

"I bet his mother stopped having kids after he was hatched."

"Have you been told today?"

"Shut your pie hole."

"You rotten, good-for-nothing @#$%&!"

"You're a total waste of skin, you loser!"

"You're a wiener/sausage with ears."

"One more word, and you're a eunuch."

"Shut up before I use my Bobbitt knife on you."

Dialogue might offer implied alternatives.

"You dirty ____."

"Did anyone ever tell you you're a ...?"

"Were you swearing at me?"

"He looks madder than Jennie last time I left the toilet seat up."

"He flipped me off. Can you believe it?"

"She gave me the bird. Then she called her divorce attorney."

"She made an obscene gesture. With both hands."

"He gave the speeder a single finger. Twice."

Exclamation points can be your friend.

Sorry, Mark Twain. You're probably cursing at me right now for what I'm about to say.

If you avoid exclamation points in your writing, readers will notice them when they *do* appear. A well-placed *!* (just one) will show intensity of emotion.

Body language and actions can speak louder than swearing.

You could make your characters:

- Flare their nostrils

- Clench their teeth

- Slam doors

- Stomp from point A to point B

- Punch holes in walls

- Prance with hands on hips

- Shake their fists

- Go red in the face

- Get so mad they stutter

- Point fingers

- Stick out their tongues

- Jut their noses in the air

- Sneer, grimace, or smirk

- Frown, pout, or purse the lips

- Raise one or both fists

- Give a thumbs-down

- Raise the palm toward someone ("talk to the hand")

- Grab the genitals

- Make a wanker gesture

- Moon someone

- Simulate a throat-slash with one finger

- Thumb the nose

Repetition dilutes impact.

Watch people in restaurants, at work, and on your commute. You might discover they don't swear as often as you think they do.

No matter what method you choose to show your characters cursing, remember that any repetition, no matter how realistic, will dilute a word or phrase's impact. Whether it's *scrutinized*, *cleared his throat*, or your favorite profanity, more than occasional occurrences will annoy your readers.

Hail the lowly grawlix.

A grawlix is a sequence of typographical symbols used to represent a non-specific profane word or phrase. A typical grawlix would be #@$%*!, which uses letters and symbols that occupy space. Carets and other skinny characters don't work as well.

Rather than insert the symbols, try sentences such as this:

He uttered a long series of scathing grawlixes.

In context, readers will know what you mean even if they're unfamiliar with the dictionary definition of *grawlix*.

Know your market when submitting to literary journals.

If your potential market offers free copies online, download and read them.

Study all guidelines. Pore through them again. And again.

Many of the alternatives provided here might be unacceptable for Christian markets. For example, some publishers might reject anything with the initials *J C* or phrases that incorporate *gosh, gee,* or *darn*—all of which are "politer" versions of *Jesus Christ, God,* and *damn.*

Check out this list.

Some of these are appropriate for young-adult or period fiction. Don't dismiss anything at first glance.

Who knows? You might invent an expression that appears in a dictionary of the future.

<u>Symbols</u>
@#$%&!

<u>A</u>
A pox upon it, arse

<u>B</u>
Balderdash, ballshirt, baloney, barf bag, barnacles, batask, beans, beeotch, bejabbers, bite me, bite my butt, blangdang, blankety-blank, blast, blast it, blasted, bleep, bleeping, blimey (Aus.), bloody, bloomin', blow(s), bologna, boogers, booty, boy-o-boy, brat, bratty, brown sugar, bug off, bullspit, bum, bummer, bunk, bunkum, burn, burned, butt hook

<u>C</u>
Chafed, chaps, cheese and crackers, cheese and rice, cheeses, cheesitz, chicken fricassee, chit, confound it, confounded, consarn, crab apples, crabby, crab cakes, crabs, crackers, crap, crapola, crappin' crackers, crappity, crappity crickets, crikey (Aus.), crimeny, cripes, crud, crumbs, cur

D

D'oh, dad gone it, dad gone thing, dad gum it, dadblameit, dadburned, daggummit, dagnabit, damned, dang, dangit, darn, darned, darnit, dastardly, dingaling, dingdong, dipstick, doggone, doggonit, donkey, donkey dung, doogee, drat, dratted, dreck-head, duckface, dumb bass dish, dump truck

E

Earwax, eat slugs, eff, effin', egad, enjoy that

F

Falderal, faq, farging, farging ice-hole, farkle, fart face, fiddle faddle, fiddlesticks, fie, fig, figgin', firetruck, fish fingers, fish sticks, flip, flip off, flippin', flippin' flapjacks, flunkin', flyin' fudgesicle, foowee, for crying out loud, for freak's sake, for Pete's sake, for the lova Mike, forklift, frack, frackin', fragdaggle, frazzle-rackin', freak, freaking, French fries, frick, frickin', frig, friggin', fuddle duddle, fudge, fudge berries, fudge nuggets, futher mucker

G

Gadzooks, garsh, gee whillikers, gee whiz, geek, geekin', geez Louise, get stuffed, glitch, glitchin', go eat a sandwich, gobbdashit, gobbledygook, golly, golly gee, good gravy, good grief, goodness, goodness gracious, gosh, goshdarnit, goshdashit, grasshole, guldurnit

H

Hail no, hay, heavens to Betsy, heavens to Murgatroyd, heck, h-e-double hockey sticks, h-e-double toothpicks, hellish, highfalutin', hockey puck, hogwash, hokey Dinah, hokey doodle, hokum, holy biscuits, holy crow, holy frijoles, holy moly, holy shibblets, holy smokes, hopping, horse feathers, horse hockey, horse pucky, huffy, hush

I

I don't give a duck, ice hole

J

Jeepers, jeepers creepers, jeez, Jiminy crickets, jive turkey, Judas Priest, jumpin' frog turds, jumpin' George, jumpin' Jiminy, just flippin' wonderful

K
Kawabunga, kitty whiskers, kung pow

L
Leapin' lizards, lint licker

M
Malarkey, man/oh man, Martha focker, Mitch, mongrel, monkey fingers, monkey flunker, mother blanker, mother fathers, mother hugger, mother of pearl, mothersmucker, mule pucky, my word

N
Nag it, nerts, no way, nonsense, nuckin' futs

O
Oh bother, omigosh

P
Peckerwood, peeves/peeved, pffft, phooey, pickle-puss, piddle, pig poop, pluck it, poo/poop/poopy, poppycock

R
Rackafratz, ram rod, raspberries, rassa-frazzin', rat doo-doo, rat dookie, rats, rice cakes, rot

S
Sack of dirt, sakes alive, San Antonio, Sasquatch, sauerkraut, schlock, shamalama, shat, shazzle, sheesh, sheet, shhugar plums, shiatsu, shinola, ship, shish kebab, shitake mushrooms, shiz, shiznit, shnikes, shoot, shucks, shush, shut the front door, sit, snails, snap, snassa-frazzin', snit, snitch, snot, son of a biscuit eater, son of a fish, son of a glitch, son of a gun, son of a mother, son of a mother trucker, son of a nutcracker, son of a pistol, sons a' guns, steaming, stink, stinkin', stuff it, stuff yourself, sucks, sufferin' succotash, sugar, sugar lumps, sunny beach, swear to my hand

T
Tartar sauce, thunderation, ticked (off), tommyrot, tool, troll, turd, turdbuckets

W
Wazzock, weenie, what the, what the blue blazes, what the duck, what the frog, what the hamfat, what the hey, what the John, when pigs fly, whillikers, whillikins, who gives a John, who gives one, who-ha, wienerwurst, witch, wow, wu-wu

Y
Yikes, you nit, yuk foo

Z
Zip it, zounds

Have

To *have*, or not to *have*? That is today's question.

As an auxiliary verb combined with a past participle, *have* forms the perfect, pluperfect, and future perfect tenses as well as the conditional mood. However, when used to express ownership, it can weaken writing.

Consider a woman in a black dress as she walks down the street. You could describe her in several ways:

She <u>had (on)</u> a black dress.
She <u>owned</u> a black dress.
She <u>paraded</u> a black dress.
She <u>wore</u> a black dress.
She <u>flaunted</u> a black dress.
She <u>modeled</u> a black dress.

Each of the preceding sentences evokes a different image, although the number of words remains static.

Analyze the following groups.

India <u>has</u> over 300,000 libraries.
India <u>boasts</u> over 300,000 libraries.
India <u>is blessed with</u> over 300,000 libraries.

Russia <u>has</u> over 17,000,000 square kilometers.
Russia <u>encompasses</u> over 17,000,000 square kilometers.
Russia <u>possesses</u> over 17,000,000 square kilometers.

Bill <u>had</u> three raw eggs before his jog.
Bill <u>gagged down</u> three raw eggs before his jog.
Bill <u>savored</u> three raw eggs before his jog.

The dog <u>had</u> a bone.
The dog <u>grappled with</u> a bone.
The dog <u>laid claim to</u> a bone.

The doctor <u>had</u> a pen behind his ear.
The doctor <u>carried</u> a pen behind his ear.
The doctor <u>stowed</u> a pen behind his ear.

Is it time to search your work in progress for all appearances of *have, has, had,* and *having*? Turn those weak spots into the excerpts that readers quote on their blogs and social media feeds.

Are you guilty of the *have-gots?*

Josie <u>has got</u> too many books.
Brent <u>had got</u> a failing grade in math.

Ouch.

Remember what your teeth feel like when you hear a train's screeching brakes? My molars are doing the grit-and-shiver routine right now.

Please never *ever* choose *have got* except in dialogue. Stick with one word or the other.

Josie <u>has</u> too many books.
Brent <u>got</u> a failing grade in math.

Better yet, find different verbs.

Josie <u>owns</u> too many books.
Brent <u>received</u> a failing grade in math.

Are you ready for a few ideas you could develop into stories?

Let's begin with the previous examples. Why does the narrator think Josie owns too many books? What caused Brent's failing math grade?

To continue, each of the following groups will begin with a generic sentence using *had*, accompanied by more interesting versions.

Brenda <u>had</u> a vast collection of dolls.

Brenda <u>hoarded</u> dolls—creepy dolls with malevolent eyes, feral teeth, and missing limbs.

206

Although the preceding sentence describes Brenda's dolls, it reveals details about her personality as well.

Brenda collected dolls—sissy dolls with long blonde locks, full eyelashes, and pouting lips.

Same character name, different dolls. Do you see a different Brenda as well?

Brenda's obsession this year? Dolls. Their beady eyes peered out of glass cases. Seventy-three tiny bodies posed as though they beseeched visitors to release them from their sterile prison.

A key phrase, *obsession this year*, shows a character who embraces fads.

Chad had eight employees.

Chad ruled over eight employees, his dictator's voice as sharp as a whip.

The words *dictator* and *whip* provide an instantaneous impression, evoking strong mental images even though Chad's appearance isn't described.

Chad managed eight employees from an office chair that never breathed fresh air unless he peeled his ponderous butt away to devour a snack from the deli next door.

This Chad comes across as an overeating slacker.

Chad boasted a staff of eight employees who never missed an opportunity to slander and sabotage one another in their quest to please him.

Here we see a Chad with a backstabbing bunch of underlings. The word *boasted* implies he supports their sabotage.

Kaya had a coffee.

Kaya clenched a huge mug of coffee, knuckles white and jaw set, while she watched the news.

Kaya's body language shows she's upset or nervous, probably about something she sees on the news.

With trembling fingers, Kaya <u>clutched</u> her coffee. One sip. Two.

What was that bitter taste?

A bitter taste? Has someone slipped drugs or poison into her brew?

Kaya <u>nurtured</u> her coffee, savoring every noisy slurp, until the last drop disappeared. She stared at the bottom of the cup. Should she call 911, or should she have another coffee first?

Why is Kaya wondering about 911? Has she found a murder victim? Maybe she's the murderer.

A good time was <u>had</u> by all.

Revelers danced, cheered, and guzzled champagne.

A sentence heavy with *tell* becomes an example of *show*. Dancing, cheering, and champagne might indicate a New Year's Eve celebration or a victory party for a political candidate.

Every guest in the audience left the live-taping with prizes and giant smiles.

Did you see a *Dr. Phil* or *Ellen* audience spilling out of the studio?

Marcel grumbled as he cleaned the floor. "Noisemakers, party hats, and barf. Looks like everyone had a great time except me."

Marcel might be the host, or he could be a disgruntled janitor.

The news broadcast <u>had</u> three anchors.

The three news anchors bickered worse than old fishwives whenever they were off-screen.

Tell becomes more *show*, but examples of the bickering would make this more engaging for readers.

Every night while Charles bellowed out local news, Andrea shuffled papers, and Dillon yawned.

Body language shows us that Andrea and Dillon may not be thrilled with Charles. *Bellowed* amplifies the discord.

Three anchors, three points of view, three identical faces. The triplets switched seats every night in a never-ending prank that kept producers and audience alike guessing at their identities.

Now we *have* a story!

Sara had three options: freeze, jump, or retreat.

In an action scene, brevity works best. The above sentence might work well on its own as long as prior passages show why Sara faces this predicament. However, brevity can be maintained while providing a more vivid picture.

Sara's toes stuck out over the narrow ledge two stories above the street. Three options scrolled before her closed eyes: freeze, jump, or retreat.

If the preceding paragraph were the first in a piece, it would set up suspense with just enough details to engage readers.

Two eagles soared below Sara's precarious perch high above the river. She teetered on the ledge as she checked her parachute. Three options whispered, wraiths in the biting wind, "Freeze, jump, or retreat."

Fate provided a fourth choice.

What is that fourth choice? Does the ledge crumble? Perhaps Sara faints. Maybe one of the eagles attacks.

This version would work best where word count is not a hindrance.

And now, the list.

Many of the preceding examples expand on ideas rather than provide direct substitutions for *have*. Replacing every instance is unrealistic, especially in micro fiction.

Scrutinize a few words and phrases you could use instead.

<u>A</u>
Accommodate, accrue, accumulate, acquire, adopt, aggregate, amass, appropriate, assemble, assume, attain

<u>B</u>
Be adorned with, be blessed with, be born with, be decorated with, be endowed with, be favored with, be in possession of, be possessed of, be privileged with, be the owner of, bear, benefit from, boast, borrow, brandish, bring, broadcast, buy

<u>C</u>
Care for, carry, clasp, clench, cling to, clutch, collect, comprise, conceal, confiscate, consume, contain, contribute, control, convey, cultivate

<u>D</u>
Defend, disclose, display, don

<u>E</u>
Enclose, encompass, endure, enjoy, exhibit, experience, expose

<u>F</u>
Fall heir to, feature, flail, flash, flaunt, flourish

<u>G</u>
Garb oneself in, garner, gather, get, get pleasure from, grab, grapple, grasp, grip

<u>H</u>
Handle, hang on to, harbor, haul, heap up, hoard, hog, hold, hold on to, hold title to, house

<u>I</u>
Imprison, include, incorporate

<u>K</u>
Keep, keep hold of, keep possession of

<u>L</u>
Latch on to, lay claim to, look after

M
Maintain, manage, manifest

N
Nurture

O
Obtain, own

P
Palm, parade, possess, procure, purchase, put on, put on display, put on view

R
Reap the benefit of, retain, reveal, rule

S
Salt away, secure, seize, shelter, show off, snaffle, sport, squirrel away, stock, stockpile, store, stow, strut, suffer, support, sustain

T
Take, take hold of, take pleasure in, teem with, transport, trumpet

U
Undergo, unveil

V
Vaunt

W
Wag, wave, wear, wield

"I" in First-Person Narration

I, I, I.

First-person narration involves people in a way they don't experience with second and third person. Readers see the world from your narrator's perspective, including intimate thoughts and feelings. However, it's easy to overplay constructions such as *I* did this and *I* thought that and *I* wanted something else.

Many people claim the *I, I, I* approach is permissible because *I* is an invisible word like *said*.

Don't believe them.

Prose or poetry with an overabundance of the same words or structures will seem off. Readers might not be able to tell you what's wrong, but they know they're unsettled by *something*.

Consider the following two story snippets.

1. I answered the irresistible beckoning of the backyard. I watched brightly colored birds there frolicking in the breeze as they fluttered toward the creek. I closed my eyes and felt the warmth of the sun. I smelled the fragrance of the clover underneath my feet, a fragrance so sweet I could almost taste it. I heard fledgling robins twittering in a nearby tree.

I thought ~~to myself~~, *This is the life.* I knew I never wanted to leave this place.

I decided to phone the real estate agent and tell her to take the FOR SALE sign off my lawn. She acted as though she had expected my call.

I told her in a firm voice that my mind was made up, and yes, I understood she would still receive her full commission.

I realized I didn't care about the money.

2. The backyard beckoned with its irresistible sights and sounds. Frolicking in the breeze, brightly colored birds fluttered toward the creek. The sun warmed my closed eyelids, and my nostrils were flooded with the sweet fragrance of clover underneath my feet, a fragrance so sweet it almost sugared the taste buds. In a nearby tree, fledgling robins twittered.

This is the life. Who in their right mind would ever leave this place?

The real estate agent acted as though she had expected my call when she was asked to take the FOR SALE sign off the lawn.

My voice was firm. "Yes, my mind is made up. ... Understood. ... You'll still receive your full commission."

Hah! Who cares about the money?

Beware verbosity.

Rewrites could result in bloat, and the wrong words could make you seem pretentious or long-winded.

The second snippet reduces, rather than increases, word count.

The first example would be even shorter with the removal of *to myself.* Who else would you think to? Your editor? Your cat? Or maybe your dictation software?

Did you notice the changes?

Almost every sentence in the first example begins with *I.*

In the rewrite, note the removal of several filtering phrases:

I watched
I ... felt
I smelled
I could ... taste
I heard
I thought
I knew
I decided
I told
I understood
I realized

Whenever you filter thoughts and senses through your narrator's eyes, you distance readers a step from your story, like a selfie of a selfie. Use the direct approach instead.

Passive voice appeared once to vary sentence structure. "I smelled the fragrance of the clover underneath my feet" became "my nostrils were flooded by the sweet fragrance of clover underneath my feet."

A so-called *rule* of writing is not to use passive voice. However, you'll find times such as this when it's warranted.

The phrase could also have been written as: "my nostrils flooded with the sweet fragrance of clover underneath my feet."

Reread the examples. Compare again. You'll notice subtle changes that make the text flow smoother.

Here's a partial list of filter words.

Watch for these or their equivalents. They all have the potential to weaken your writing:

Assume, be able to, believe, can, decide, experience, feel (or feel like), hear, know, look, note, notice, realize, remember, see, seem, sound (or sound like), taste, think, touch, watch, wonder

Change the focus.

Just because you're writing in first person doesn't mean you, the storyteller, should be the most important character in the piece.

If you concentrate on the activities of other characters, readers will feel as though they are you. They still know you're the narrator, but you become invisible.

Here are a few examples of *I* alternatives.

- I agree: We are in agreement.

- I am convinced that: In my opinion.

- I am sure that: Correct me if my opinion is wrong.

- I believe: The experts say (or, in *Dothraki*, "It is known.")

- I decided: It was my intention.

- I disagree: You are wrong.

- I dislike that: That's not for me.

- I don't know: That's an excellent question.

- I feel: In light of the evidence.

- I have experience in: My experience includes.

- I interpret the results: The results indicate.

- I like: It's one of my favorites.

- I was nearly hit by a car: A car nearly hit me.

- I'll show you: The report will show you.

- I'm hungry: My stomach is growling.

Beware the *me-my* snare.

In an attempt to remove instances of *I,* you might introduce excessive repetition of *me* and *my.*

For instance, "I felt an irresistible urge to buy the shoes" could become "An irresistible urge to buy the shoes came over me."

"I saw three chickadees sitting on the fence" could end up as "Three chickadees sitting on the fence came into ~~my~~ view."

As shown by the strikeout, you can often omit *my.*

Your ears are excellent critics.

Read your text out loud or harness your computer's text-to-speech capabilities and listen to your writing. Repetitions that hide from notice during a silent read often become obvious and irritating when processed by the ears.

Redundancies

Redundant words, or pleonasms, are a misery for many writers.

This chapter presents over 400 common redundancies. Avoid them, and your writing will benefit.

Why should you remove redundant words?

- They bloat writing, an obstacle if your word count is limited.

- They make your work difficult to digest. If a person can't read a sentence out loud without struggling for breath, redundant words might be the problem.

- Some redundancies make you appear pompous. Do you want your work to read like legalese or purple prose?

- Pleonasms detract from the quality and coherency of your writing.

- Redundancies are by definition superfluous. They dilute rather than augment, forcing readers to wade through useless text.

Analyze determiners.

You can often delete determiners without changing the meaning of the text. If you need to show degrees of intensity, select stronger verbs or adjectives.

Consider these two paragraphs.

Truthfully, the sun was horribly hot. Honestly. It burnt me really bad.

As dialogue, the previous paragraph might work. However, let's pick it apart. Would somebody speak untruthfully? Scrap *truthfully*. Ditto for *honestly*. Even if readers swallow the first affirmation of truthfulness, the second will be too much. A *really bad* sunburn would cause blisters. Consider this more concise version:

The scorching sun gave me a blistering sunburn.

Scrutinize your writing for the following words and their relatives. Do you need them?

Actually, almost, basically, definitely, especially, essentially, extremely, fairly, generally, genuinely, honestly, incredibly, intensely, just, kind of, moderately, only, particularly, quite, rather, really, significantly, slightly, somewhat, sort of, specifically, such, truthfully, type of, very

Do you fall into this redundancy trap?

Analyze the following sentences.

Ricky began to dream of lollipops and candy canes.

Mrs. Brown started to wash the floor.

Rufus began to gnaw on a bone.

Georgina started brushing her hair.

Each sentence shows a character commencing an action. Do they begin doing something, or do they just *do* it?

These versions produce stronger writing:

Ricky dreamt of lollipops and candy canes.

Mrs. Brown washed the floor.

Rufus gnawed on a bone.

Georgina brushed her hair.

The second group of sentences contains fewer words, and the action is more direct.

You can usually omit all forms of *begin* and *start* in your writing. That includes synonyms such as *commence, instigate,* and *initiate.*

That, that, that. How often do you use *that?*

Most of us can trim our word count by searching our writing for *that.* You don't believe me? I'll prove it.

I know that you're a writer; otherwise you wouldn't have decided that you wanted to buy this book. I hope that you find it helpful. I know that many of these lists have assisted me.

Ugh. Four occurrences of *that* in a single paragraph. Time for a rewrite.

I know you're a writer; otherwise you wouldn't have decided to buy this book. I hope you find it helpful. I know many of these lists have assisted me.

Not a single *that* in the second version, and with some minor revision, the paragraph went from thirty-five words to twenty-nine.

Do you use some of the following phrases?

If you doubt anything you see in the following pages, check your dictionary.

Let's consider *kneel ~~down~~.*

Kneel: to go <u>down</u> and rest on the knees or a knee

The definition of *kneel* already includes *down.*

Embrace the same approach for other entries, remembering that dialogue is an exception to the rule. People speak with redundant phrases, and your characters should sound realistic.

<u>Numeric</u>
3 a.m. ~~in the morning~~
4 p.m. ~~at night~~
~~12~~ midnight
~~12~~ noon

<u>A</u>
~~a total of~~ 5,280
~~absolutely~~ certain
~~absolutely~~ committed
~~absolutely~~ essential
~~absolutely~~ necessary
~~absolutely~~ the worst
~~actual~~ facts

add ~~an additional~~
add ~~up~~
~~added~~ bonus
advance ~~forward~~
~~advance~~ planning
~~advance~~ reservations
~~advance~~ warning
~~aid and~~ abet
AIDS ~~syndrome~~
all ~~of~~
all ~~of them~~
~~all things considered~~
~~all~~ throughout
~~all-time~~ record
alternative ~~choice~~
~~annual~~ anniversary
~~anonymous~~ stranger
~~armed~~ gunman
~~artificial~~ prosthesis
~~as a matter of fact~~
~~as far as I'm concerned~~
~~as~~ yet
ascend ~~up~~
ask ~~a question~~
assemble ~~together~~
ATM ~~machine~~
attach ~~together~~

<u>B</u>
bald-~~headed~~
balsa ~~wood~~
~~basic~~ essentials
~~basic~~ fundamentals
~~basic~~ necessities
because ~~of the fact that~~
best ~~ever~~
biography ~~of a person's life~~
blend ~~together~~
blink ~~at~~
blue/gold/red, etc. ~~in color~~
both ~~of them~~

~~brand~~ new
brief ~~in duration~~
~~brief~~ moment
~~brief~~ summary
~~burning~~ embers
~~but~~ nevertheless
but ~~nevertheless~~

C
cacophony ~~of sound~~
cancel ~~out~~
~~careful~~ scrutiny
cash ~~money~~
cease ~~and desist~~
CEO ~~officer~~
chai ~~tea~~
circle ~~around~~
circulate ~~around~~
clap ~~one's hands~~
clap ~~one's hands together~~
classify ~~into groups~~
clench ~~hard~~
climb ~~up~~
~~close~~ proximity
~~closed~~ fist
CMS ~~system~~
collaborate ~~together~~
combine ~~together~~
commute ~~back and forth~~
compete ~~with each other~~
~~complete~~ opposite
~~completely~~ annihilate
~~completely~~ destroy
~~completely~~ different
~~completely~~ eliminate
~~completely~~ engulf
~~completely~~ finish
~~completely~~ full
~~completely~~ surround
~~completely~~ unanimous
~~component~~ parts

confer ~~together~~
connect ~~together~~
connect ~~up~~
consensus ~~of opinion~~
~~constantly~~ maintained
continue ~~on~~
cooperate ~~together~~
could ~~possibly~~
CPU ~~unit~~
~~crack of~~ dawn
crisis ~~situation~~
cross the arms ~~over the chest~~
crouch ~~down~~
~~crystal~~-clear
~~current~~ trend
~~currently~~ away

D
~~dead~~ serious
~~definite~~ decision
depreciate ~~in value~~
descend ~~down~~
~~desirable~~ benefit
~~diametrically~~ opposed
different ~~kinds~~
~~difficult~~ dilemma
~~direct~~ confrontation
disappear ~~from sight~~
~~dog-eat-dog~~ fierce competition
dress ~~up~~ in
drop ~~down~~
during ~~the course of~~
dwindle ~~down~~

E
~~each and~~ every
each ~~and every~~
earlier ~~in time~~
echo ~~back~~
eliminate ~~altogether~~
eliminate ~~entirely~~

emergency ~~situation~~
~~empty~~ hole
empty ~~out~~
~~empty~~ space
enclosed ~~herewith/herein~~
~~end~~ result
enter ~~into~~
~~entirely~~ different
~~entirely~~ eliminate
equal ~~to one another~~
eradicate ~~completely~~
estimated at ~~about~~
every ~~single~~ person
evolve ~~over time~~
~~exact~~ same
~~exactly~~ the same
~~exposed~~ opening
extradite ~~back~~

F

~~face~~ mask
face ~~up to~~ the facts
fall ~~down~~
~~false~~ pretense
~~favorable~~ approval
~~fellow~~ classmate
~~fellow~~ colleague
few ~~in number~~
filled ~~to capacity~~
~~final~~ completion
~~final~~ end
~~final~~ outcome
~~final~~ solution
~~final~~ ultimatum
~~first and~~ foremost
~~first~~ conceived
first ~~of all~~
five ~~in number~~
fly ~~through the air~~
focus ~~in~~ on
follow ~~after~~

for all intents and purposes

~~for all intents and purposes~~
~~for the most part~~
~~foreign~~ imports
forever ~~and ever~~
~~former~~ graduate
~~former~~ veteran
~~free~~ gift
~~from~~ whence
~~frozen~~ ice
~~frozen~~ tundra
~~full~~ satisfaction
full ~~to capacity~~
fuse ~~together~~
~~future~~ plans
~~future~~ recurrence

G
gather ~~together~~
~~general~~ public
~~give a~~ gasp
~~give a~~ nod
~~give a~~ shrug
~~give a~~ sigh
~~give a~~ smile
~~give~~ voice ~~to~~
~~go and~~ get
GOP ~~party~~
GRE ~~exam~~
grind the jaw ~~from side to side~~
grow ~~in size~~

H
hand ~~down~~
~~harmful~~ injuries
has ~~got~~
have ~~got~~
he is ~~someone~~ from
~~head~~ honcho
heat ~~up~~
her ~~own~~
~~hidden~~ ambush

his ~~own~~
HIV ~~virus~~
hoist ~~up~~
~~hollow~~ tube
~~honestly~~
~~hopeful~~ optimism
~~hot~~ water heater
~~hot-dog~~ show-off
HPV ~~virus~~
hurry ~~up~~

I
I am ~~currently~~ a
I saw it ~~with my own eyes~~
I thought ~~to myself~~
~~illustrated~~ drawing
~~in a manner of speaking~~
~~in a very real sense~~
in close ~~proximity~~
~~in my opinion~~
~~in the final analysis~~
in the ~~general~~ vicinity
~~in the process of~~
in the same proximity ~~to each other~~
incredible ~~to believe~~
inside ~~of~~ (position)
integrate ~~together~~
integrate ~~with each other~~
interdependent ~~on each other~~
introduced ~~for the first time~~
ISBN ~~number~~
it is ~~after all~~
~~it was back~~ in 2013 ~~when~~
it's ~~literally~~ impossible
it's not that big ~~of~~ a deal

J
join ~~together~~
~~joint~~ collaboration

K
kneel ~~down~~
know ~~that~~
~~knowledgeable~~ experts

L
lag ~~behind~~
laminate ~~together~~
large ~~in size~~
largest ~~ever~~
later ~~time~~
LCD ~~display~~
lift ~~up~~
~~live~~ witness
longer ~~in length~~
look ~~ahead~~ to the future
look back ~~in retrospect~~

M
made ~~out~~ of
~~major~~ breakthrough
~~major~~ feat
manually ~~by hand~~
~~material~~ success
may/might ~~possibly~~
meet ~~together~~
meet ~~up~~
meet ~~with each other~~
~~mental~~ attitude
~~mental~~ telepathy
merge ~~together~~
miles apart ~~from one another~~
mix ~~together~~
MLB ~~baseball~~
more ~~and more~~
~~more~~ perfect
most ~~of the~~ people
~~most~~ unique
moving ~~experience~~
~~mutual~~ cooperation
mutual respect ~~for each other~~

my ~~own~~
my ~~personal~~ opinion

N
nape ~~of the neck~~
narrow ~~down~~
~~native~~ habitat
~~natural~~ instinct
near ~~to~~
never ~~before~~
~~new~~ innovation
~~new~~ invention
~~new~~ recruit
NFL ~~league~~
nod ~~the head~~
none ~~at all~~
nostalgia ~~for the past~~
~~now~~ pending
~~number one~~ leader

O
oak ~~wood~~
off ~~of~~
~~open~~ trench
open ~~up~~
~~oral~~ conversation
~~originally~~ created
~~outside~~ in the yard
outside ~~of~~
oval ~~in shape~~
~~over~~ exaggerate
over ~~with~~
~~overused~~ cliché

P
~~pair of~~ twins
palm ~~of the hand~~
~~passing~~ fad
~~past~~ experience
~~past~~ history
~~past~~ memories

past~~ records
penetrate ~~into~~
~~period of~~ four days
~~personal~~ friend
~~personal~~ opinion
pick ~~and choose~~
PIN ~~number~~
pine ~~wood~~
pizza ~~pie~~
plan ~~ahead~~
plan ~~in advance~~
~~please~~ RSVP
plunge ~~down~~
point ~~one's finger~~
~~polar~~ opposites
~~positive~~ identification
postpone ~~until later~~
pouring ~~down~~ rain
~~present~~ incumbent
present ~~time~~
previously listed ~~above~~
proceed ~~ahead~~
protest ~~against~~
protruded ~~out~~
puppy ~~dog~~
pursue ~~after~~
push the envelope ~~too far~~
puzzling ~~in nature~~

R

raise ~~up~~
RAM ~~memory~~
reach ~~out~~
~~really~~ overstate
reason ~~why~~
recall ~~to mind~~
recheck ~~again~~
reconnect ~~back~~
rectangular ~~in shape~~
recur ~~again~~
redo ~~again~~

re-elect ~~for another term~~
refer ~~back~~
reflect ~~back~~
~~regular~~ routine
repeat ~~again~~
reply ~~back~~
retreat ~~back~~
return ~~again~~
revert ~~back~~
review ~~again~~
~~ripe~~ old age
rise ~~up~~
roll ~~over~~ onto
round ~~in shape~~

S

~~safe~~ haven
~~safe~~ sanctuary
said ~~before~~
said ~~previously~~
same ~~exact~~
same ~~identical~~
scream ~~loudly~~
scrutinize ~~in detail~~
seize ~~hold of~~
~~separate and~~ apart
separate ~~and apart~~
separated ~~apart~~
~~serious~~ danger
share ~~together~~
~~sharp~~ point
shine ~~down~~ on the floor
shiny ~~in appearance~~
shorter ~~in length~~
shrug ~~the shoulders~~
shut ~~down~~
sigh ~~of relief~~
sign up ~~for~~ free
since ~~the time that~~
sing ~~out~~
~~single~~ unit

sit ~~down~~
skip ~~over~~
skirt ~~around~~
slow ~~speed~~
small ~~in size~~
~~small~~ speck
smile ~~to oneself~~
~~sneaking~~ suspicion
soft ~~to the touch~~
sole ~~of the foot~~
spell out ~~in detail~~
spliced ~~together~~
square ~~in shape~~
stand ~~up~~
start ~~off~~
start ~~out~~
~~still~~ persists
~~still~~ remains
stretch ~~out~~
~~sudden~~ impulse
~~suddenly~~ exploded
~~sum~~ total
~~summarily~~ dismiss
summarize ~~briefly~~
surrounded ~~on all sides~~
~~surrounding~~ circumstances
swirl ~~up~~ into the sky

T
~~take a~~ look at
~~take a~~ taste
take ~~over~~ to
tall ~~in height/stature~~
tap ~~gently~~
~~tell a~~ lie
~~temper~~ tantrum
~~tend to~~ avoid
~~the~~ both of us
the ~~exact~~ opposite
the fact ~~of the matter~~ is
the future ~~to come~~

the ~~immediate~~ short-term
~~the point is that~~
the reason is ~~because~~
the reason ~~why~~
the time ~~when~~
the ~~very~~ latest
their ~~own~~
their ~~own personal~~
their ~~own unique~~ personalities
then ~~and there~~
~~therapeutic~~ treatment
~~there are~~ many ~~who~~ think
~~there is~~ a man ~~who~~
~~there is~~ no one ~~who~~
they ~~all~~
thin ~~out~~
~~three~~ triplets
~~three-way~~ love triangle
tilt the head ~~sideways~~
~~tiny~~ bit/speck
~~to coin a phrase~~
~~to make a long story short~~
~~to tell the truth~~
~~total~~ destruction
~~totally~~ free
~~totally~~ unique
touch ~~gently~~
~~true~~ facts
~~truly~~ sincere
tuna ~~fish~~
turn ~~about~~
turn ~~around~~
~~two equal~~ halves
~~two~~ twins

U
~~ultimate~~ goal
undergraduate ~~student~~
~~underground~~ subway
~~unexpected~~ emergency
~~unexpected~~ surprise

~~unintentional~~ mistake
~~universal~~ panacea
until ~~such time as~~
UPC ~~code~~
~~usual~~ custom

V

vacillate ~~back and forth~~
~~verbally~~ said
~~very~~ beginning
~~very~~ end
~~very~~ long ~~period of~~ time
~~very~~ outset
visible ~~to the eye~~

W

wake ~~up~~
~~wall~~ mural
warn ~~in advance~~
weather ~~conditions~~
weather ~~situation~~
~~what I mean to say is~~
~~what~~ it ~~all amounts to~~ is
what ~~it is~~ you need
what ~~it is that~~
~~what~~ that means ~~is~~
~~when I think about it~~
whether ~~or not~~
whirl ~~around~~
whisper ~~softly~~
~~white~~ snow
why ~~it is~~
write ~~down~~

Y

yell ~~loudly~~
your ~~own~~

Rolling the Eyes

Should you ever make your characters roll their eyes?

To *roll the eyes* is a commonly used idiom. Many editors don't like it, insisting that the expression makes readers envision eyes rolling across the floor like marbles. However, people understand what a writer means by the phrase. In my opinion, editors' biases are old-fashioned, and I was born when dinosaurs still roamed the Earth.

Having said that, rolling of the eyes is cliché, best reserved for dialogue and children's or young adult books. Nevertheless, even in books written for kids, overuse of any expression is taboo.

Effective dialogue can help.

Anything a person would say in real life a writer can repeat in written dialogue. Note how the following snippets of speech include the dreaded idiom in a way that won't offend your editor.

"Don't you roll your eyes at me, you insensitive jerk."

"If you don't smarten up, I'm gonna take those rolling eyes and use 'em for marbles."

"You got a problem? Maybe I should glue your eyes in place to keep them from rolling around that empty space inside your head."

Why do your characters need to roll their eyes?

If you understand motivations, you can substitute suitable body language.

Rolling the eyes could indicate:

Annoyance, boredom, contempt, disbelief, impatience, nonchalance, sarcasm, scorn, skepticism, smugness

Consider alternative ways to show the above emotions.

Annoyance
Tapping foot
Clenched jaw
Crossed arms
Throbbing vein in the neck

Boredom
Sighing
Drumming fingers
Lethargic movements
Unfocussed gaze or staring

Contempt
Sneering
Snorting
Pinched lips
Stuck-out tongue

Disbelief
Gaping mouth
Inability to speak
Rapid blinking
Widened eyes

Impatience
Pacing
Tapping one's foot
Watching a clock or wristwatch
Hair-twirling or other habitual behaviors

Nonchalance
Joking
Shrugging
Cheesy grin
Changing the subject

Sarcasm
Overstatement
Uneven smile
Raised eyebrows
Statements with double meanings

Scorn
Crossed arms
Wrinkled nose
Dismissive hand gesture
Tightening of the upper lip

Skepticism
Shrugging
Shaking the head
Condescending smile
Muttering disagreement

Smugness
Rocking on heels
Blustering speech
Strutting or swaggering
Leaning toward another character, invading their personal space

Try sentences like the following:

She propped her hands on her hips and gave him a look that told him he'd be sleeping on the couch again.

His eyes bulged so much they looked like billiard balls.

She screwed her face into a grimace that reminded him of his neighbor's pug.

He curled his lip and stared at the ceiling.

Let your characters *tell*.

They know how they're feeling in the moment and can reveal their emotions via dialogue or internal sensations.

"Do you really mean that, or are you full of baloney? As usual."

"Yeah, right. That's never gonna happen."

She gave me a dismissive blink that made me feel like an insect.

Jolene's flirtations annoyed Jim more than his mother's incessant nagging.

Shirley's impatience filled her with a suppressed urge to tap her foot as she waited for Bill to finish his lame joke.

Try direct alternatives for *roll the eyes.*

When you need something concise, this list might provide what you're looking for.

<u>B</u>
Bait, balk, belittle, bellyache, berate, blink, bluster, bridle, bristle

<u>C</u>
Chaff, challenge, clown around, complain, cringe, criticize, cut up

<u>D</u>
Demur, deride, disdain, disparage, dissent, dodge

<u>F</u>
Flinch, frown

<u>G</u>
Gape, gawk, gawp, give a start, glare, glower, goad, goggle, grimace, gripe, grouch, grouse, grumble

<u>H</u>
Harrumph

<u>I</u>
Insult

<u>J</u>
Jeer, jest, joke, josh

<u>K</u>
Kid around

<u>L</u>
Leer, look askance, look sideways

<u>M</u>
Make a face, make fun of, moan, mock, mumble, mutter

N
Narrow the eyes

O
Object

P
Pace, poke fun at, pooh-pooh, pout, protest, provoke, pull a face

R
Rag, raise the eyebrows, rant, razz, rebuff, recoil, revile, rib, ridicule

S
Scoff, scorn, scowl, shrug, sigh, simper, smirk, sneer, snicker, snigger, snort, snuffle, spurn, stiffen, suck the teeth

T
Taunt, tease, titter, tsk-tsk, twit

W
Whine, whinge, wince

To Be

Why should you avoid *to be* in its various forms?

William Shakespeare's Hamlet said, "To be or not to be, that is the question."

Centuries later, writers face the same dilemma.

To be is an integral part of everyday speech. It exists for a reason. However, this verb can cause lackluster writing if overused.

Here's an easy fix for phrases that start with *there*.

You can often omit *there is*, *there was*, *there were*, and *there will be* with minor changes in capitalization and punctuation. Whenever possible, choose stronger verbs.

~~There is~~ no doubt ~~that~~ ...
No doubt ...

~~There is~~ no method ~~that~~ is guaranteed to succeed.
No method <u>guarantees</u> success.

~~There was~~ a man ~~who~~ had a horse.
A man <u>owned</u> a horse.

~~There was~~ one child ~~who~~ got measles.
One child <u>contracted</u> measles.

~~There are~~ many weeds ~~that~~ overwinter.
Many weeds overwinter.

~~There are~~ many voters ~~who~~ are sick of the candidates' attacks.
Many voters <u>find</u> the candidates' attacks disgusting.

~~There will be~~ many ~~who~~ disagree.
Many will disagree.

~~There will be~~ several lectures ~~that~~ explain redundancies.
Several lectures will explain redundancies.

Active verbs strengthen your writing.

The right verb can show in one word what might take several phrases to express otherwise.

Which is more direct?

I am a writer. OR *I write.*

I am the one who cares. OR *I care.*

In the second of each preceding example, the word count diminishes, and the sentence becomes more active.

The lion was behind the tree.

Why was the lion behind the tree? Was he having a nap? Stalking prey? Basking in the sunshine?

The lion <u>hid</u> behind the tree.

Now we have a sentence that adds to the story.

The toddler was in the bathtub.

Why? Was the child taking a bath? Hiding from Mommy? Drowning?

The toddler <u>cowered</u> in the bathtub.

With one simple edit, we see the makings of a story.

There was an eagle in the sky.

Unimaginative.

An eagle <u>soared</u> across the sky.

Can you see the eagle?

Continuous tense weakens your writing.

Continuous is formed by combining *to be* with the present participle (*-ing* form) of another verb. You may find occasions where continuous works best for you, but examine every instance.

Scrutinize the following examples. In most cases, the second sentence is stronger.

I am strolling.
I stroll.

I was rowing the boat.
I rowed the boat.

I will be attending the recital.
I will attend the recital.

He is ogling the girls on the street.
He ogles the girls on the street.

She was dancing and twirling.
She danced and twirled.

He will be singing a solo.
He will sing a solo.

They are laughing at him.
They laugh at him.

The kids were swimming without water wings.
The kids swam without water wings.

They will be working all weekend.
They will work all weekend.

Occupations represent more than labels.

Instead of naming a person's occupation, show it.

He is a mechanic.
He repairs Fords.

She is a gourmet chef.
She makes the best crème brûlée in town.

He is a teacher.
He teaches physics.

She is a doctor.
She specializes in internal medicine.

He is a pilot.
He pilots his own twin-engine Cessna Citation.

She is a writer.
She writes horror fiction.

Review more examples.

His features were a network of wrinkles and spots.
A network of wrinkles and spots <u>obscured</u> his features.

Two boats were in the water.
Two boats <u>floated</u> in the water.

Gerald was in the yard.
Gerald <u>dawdled</u> in the yard.

Fifty guests were in the room.
Fifty guests <u>wedged</u> into the room.

The flowers were in the vase.
The flowers <u>wilted</u> in the vase.

There were ants on the sandwich.
Ants <u>swarmed</u> the sandwich.

There were leaves in the gutters.
Leaves <u>choked</u> the gutters.

He was in the hallway.
He <u>loitered</u> in the hallway.

The preceding examples draw on verbs from the following list.

Try these active replacements for *to be* in past tense.

They represent only a few of the thousands you could choose.

<u>A</u>
Abided/abode, assembled

<u>B</u>
Balanced, basked, bent, blanketed, blocked, burrowed

<u>C</u>
Choked, collected, colonized, convened, covered, cowered, cozied up, crammed, crouched, crowded, curled up

<u>D</u>
Dawdled, dozed, drooped

<u>E</u>
Existed

<u>F</u>
Filled, floated, flocked, flooded

<u>G</u>
Gathered

<u>H</u>
Harbored, heaped, hid, hovered, huddled, hung around

<u>I</u>
Idled, inhabited, inundated

<u>J</u>
Jammed

<u>K</u>
Knelt

<u>L</u>
Lay, lazed, lined, lingered, lived, lodged, lolled, lounged

<u>M</u>
Massed, met, milled, mounded

N
Nested, nestled

O
Occupied

P
Packed, perched, piled, poised, populated, posed, postured

R
Ranged, reclined, relaxed, remained, reposed, resided, rested, reunited, roomed, roosted

S
Sagged, sat, saturated, settled, sheltered, shrouded, slept, slouched, slumbered, slumped, snoozed, sojourned, sprawled, spread-eagled, squeezed, squished, stacked, stayed, stood, stooped, stretched out, stuck, sunned, swamped, swarmed

T
Teemed, tenanted, thronged

U
Unwound

W
Waited, wallowed, wedged, wilted

Sensory Words

Our world floods us with sensations. If you describe a scene without adding scent, sound, taste, temperature, and texture, it will come across like a stick-figure drawing.

This section of the book offers a few ways to turn your writing into a multidimensional art form that will engross readers.

Hearing: Onomatopoeic Sound Words

Well-chosen sounds give writing more *oomph*.

Writers can describe sounds, or they can choose verbs and nouns that do the same, often with fewer words.

Dictionary.com defines onomatopoeia as:

"the formation of a word ... by imitation of a sound made by or associated with its referent;

"a word so formed;

"the use of imitative and naturally suggestive words for rhetorical, dramatic, or poetic effect."

Which sentences in the following pairs stimulate your sense of hearing better?

The toy train ran over the tiny track and fell off at the last corner.

The toy train clickety-clacked over the tiny track and rattled off at the last corner.

Can you hear the train in the second sentence?

I heard the doorbell and went to the door to see who it was.

The doorbell chimed, and I shuffled to the door to see who it was.

The second example, rather than filter through the narrator's senses, transmits the sound of the doorbell directly to readers' ears. *Shuffled* shows that the narrator moves slowly to the door.

The heavy rain poured through a crack in the roof.

The rain gushed through a crack in the roof.

Gushed shows the heavy rain. Do you hear it?

Two books fell to the floor.

Two books <u>thudded</u> to the floor.

Thudded, as well as adding sound, implies that the books are heavy. I could have used *fluttered* or *rustled* for lighter books.

She never shut up. It drove me crazy.

Her <u>yammering</u> drove me crazy.

A *yammer* is a whining or complaining voice, loud and sustained or repetitive.

The coyote looked in my direction when I stepped on the twigs.

When the twigs <u>snapped</u> under my feet, the coyote <u>yipped</u> in my direction.

Although *looked* and *yipped* aren't interchangeable, perhaps *yipped* is a better verb choice. Snapping twigs demonstrate why the coyote's attention focuses on the narrator. Moving the twigs to the beginning of the sentence shows cause and effect in the correct order.

The toddler made cute little noises as he bathed.

The toddler <u>babbled</u> and <u>splashed</u> in the bathtub.

Besides omitting overused words *cute* and *little*, the second sentence brims with sound.

In an inventive mood? Check the internet first.

Words that stimulate your auditory sense could convey an offensive undertone in English or another language.

For instance, *whoppa-whoppa* might seem like a good sound to use for helicopter blades. However, a Google search shows it would be an inappropriate choice.

More examples and story prompts follow.

Edit these at will and feel free to capitalize on them for story starters.

1. The robot rumbled through the lobby, blipping and blooping, until it reached the reception desk. "Pardon me, ma'am," it droned, "could you direct me to the presidential suite?"

2. A stalactite over Tom's head drip-drip-dripped. Invisible wings whirred by his face, stirring the fetid odor of mold and bat guano. He strained at his fetters and screamed.

3. A chittering chipmunk scurried over the firepit toward the bird feeder. A blue jay fluttered away, squawking its disapproval. The chipmunk scratched and scrabbled in the feeder until it found what it was looking for: a glittering blue gem.

4. A deafening boom drowned the screech of the train's brakes as it hit the car. Locomotive and auto locked in a tangled embrace, metal on metal, groaning forward in a spray of sparks.

5. The fraying rope vibrated under Doug's feet as he slid forward, too terrified to peek into the ravine below. A breeze wafted hair into his face and swelled into a gust that nearly toppled him over. His anxious inhalations turned into gasps of panic.

6. Sylvan yelped when the snake slithered down his shoulder and into his shirt. One thwack. Two. A hiss rewarded his efforts, and fangs scissored into the folds of his belly. He flopped onto the floor, continuing his frenzied yips as he walloped the poisonous monster.

7. The Great Beltazinni thumped the false bottom of the dollhouse. Three cooing doves materialized. They flittered across the stage and over the clapping audience, plopping bird poop onto shoulders and heads; and nobody noticed when Beltazinni's accomplices slipped their fingers into purses and pockets.

The list that will stimulate your ears.

Most of the following words will function as either nouns or verbs. By adding *ing*, you can also turn them into adjectives.

<u>A</u>
Achoo, ahem, ahoy, arf, argh, awk

B

Baa, babble, bada-boom, bam, bang, barf, bark, baroom, bash, bawl, bay, bazinga, beep, belch, bellow, biff, bing, blab, blam, blare, blast, blat, bleat, bleep, blip, bloop, blop, blub, blurp, bluster, boff, boing, boink, bong, bonk, boo, boo-hoo, boom, boop, bop, bow-wow, brat-a-tat, bray, brring, bubble, bump, burble, burp, burr, buzz, bwah-ha-ha, bwak

C

Cackle, caterwaul, caw, cha-ching, champ, chatter, cheep, chime, chirp, chirr, chirrup, chitter, chomp, choo-choo, chug, chunk, clack, clackety-clack, clang, clank, clap, clash, clatter, click, clickety-clack, clink, clip-clop, clippity-clop, cluck, clunk, cock-a-doodle-doo, coo, cough, crack, crackle, crash, creak, crinkle, croak, croon, crow, crunch, cuckoo

D

D'oh, ding, ding-dong, doink, doo-wop, dribble, drip, drip-drop, drone, drum, duh

E

Echo, eek, eeyowch, erp

F

Fizz, fizzle, flap, flick, flip-flop, flit, flitter, flush, flutter, fwap

G

Gag, gaggle, gak, gallop, gargle, gasp, gibber, glub, glug, gnash, gnaw, gobble, gong, grate, grind, groan, growl, grr, grumble, grump, grunt, guffaw, gulp, gurgle, gush, gust

H

Hack, har-har, harrumph, haw, hawk, hee-haw, hee-hee, heh-heh, hem, hey, hiccup, hiss, hock, ho-ho, ho-hum, holler, honk, hooray, hoot, howl, huff, hum, hush, hyuk-hyuk

I

Jabber, jangle, jingle

K

Kaboom, ka-ching, kapow, kerplunk, klunk, knack, knock, kwok

L
Lap, lisp, low

M
Meow, mew, moan, moo, mrow, mumble, murmur, mutter, mwa-ha-ha

N
Natter, neener-neener, neigh, nicker, nyah-nyah

O
Oink, ooh, oompah, ouch

P
Pant, patter, peel, peep, pfft, pfoom, phew, phooey, ping, ping-pong, pip, pitter-patter, plink, plonk, plop, plunk, pock, poof, pooh-pooh, pop, pound, pow, prattle, psst, puff, pulse, purr, putt-putt

Q
Quack, quaver

R
Rap, rasp, rat-a-tat, rattle, rawr, ribbet, ring, rip, roar, rub-a-dub, ruff, rumble, rush, rustle

S
Scissor, screak, scream, screech, scritch, scrunch, scurry, shoo, shriek, shuffle, shush, sizzle, skid, skirl, slam, slash, slip, slither, slop, slurp, smack, smash, snap, snarl, sneeze, snick, sniff, sniffle, snip, snore, snort, snuffle, sob, splash, splat, splatter, splish, sploosh, splosh, splut, splutter, spoing, spray, sputter, squawk, squeak, squeal, squee, squelch, squish, stamp, stomp, strum, swash, swish, swoosh

T
Ta-da, tap, tee-hee, throb, thrum, thud, thump, thunder, thung, thunk, thwack, thwip, thwok, tick-tock, ting, tinkle, titter, toot, trill, trumpet, tsk-tsk, tut-tut, twang, tweet, twitter, twit-twoo, tzing

U
Umpa

V

Viip, voomp, vroom, vzzzt

W

Waa, waft, wahoo, wah-wah, wail, wallop, wap-wap-wap, warble, waul, wawl, whack, whacka-whacka, wham, whang, whap, whee, wheeze, whiff, whimper, whine, whinny, whirr, whish, whisper, whistle, whock, whomp, whoop, whoosh, whop, whump, wicker, woof, woo-hoo, wub-wub, wuppa-wuppa

Y

Yackety-yack, yabber, yadda-yadda, yahoo, yammer, yap, yaup, yawp, yee-haw, yelp, yeow, yip, yoo-hoo, yowl

Z

Zap, zing, zip, zonk, zoom, zzz

Sight: Color Words

Why is color in writing so important?

Pablo Picasso said that "Colors, like features, follow the changes of the emotions." Picasso was an artist who evoked emotion with colorful pigments. As a writer, you can do the same with colorful words.

Note the different pictures painted by the following two paragraphs.

Ned gazed at the calypso-orange horizon. A lapis-blue speck sparkled above it in the deepening violet of a new night sky—Planet Vorton, home.

Ned gaped at the corpse-grey horizon. A mold-blue speck festered above it in the deepening black of a smoggy night sky—Planet Vorton, home.

Same number of words, different colors, with complementing adjectives and verbs. One paragraph emanates optimism, the other gloom.

Compound adjectives sometimes require hyphens.

As mentioned in a previous chapter, *The Chicago Manual of Style* says that compound adjectives before a noun should be hyphenated.

Compare the following examples:

*Tristan wore an **eye-catching** purple tie.*
*Tristan's purple tie was **eye catching**.*

*Wendi modeled a **melon-pink** dress.*
*Wendi's dress was **melon pink**.*

Accent colors with adjectives.

Here's a list over one hundred adjectives from thousands you could choose to produce more vivid descriptions of the colors in your writing.

A
Accented, achromatic, ashen, ashy, atomic

B
Blazing, bleached, bleak, blinding, blotchy, bold, brash, bright, brilliant, burnt

C
Chromatic, classic, clean, cold, complementing, contrasting, cool, coordinating, creamy, crisp, crystalline

D
Dark, dayglow, dazzling, deep, delicate, digital, dim, dirty, drab, dreary, dull, dusty

E
Earthy, electric, energetic, eye-catching

F
Faded, faint, festive, fiery, flashy, flattering, fluorescent, frosty, full-toned

G
Gaudy, glistening, glittering, glossy, glowing

H
Harsh, hazy, hot

I
Icy, illuminated, incandescent, intense, iridescent

K
Knockout

L
Lambent, light, loud, luminous, lusterless, lustrous

M
Majestic, matte, medium, mellow, milky, monochromatic, muddy, murky, muted

<u>N</u>
Natural, neon, neutral

<u>O</u>
Opalescent, opaque

<u>P</u>
Pale, pastel, patchy, pearly, perfect, picturesque, plain, primary, pure

<u>R</u>
Radiant, reflective, rich, royal, ruddy, rustic

<u>S</u>
Satiny, saturated, shaded, sheer, shining, shiny, shocking, showy, smoky, soft, solid, somber, soothing, sooty, sparkling, stained, streaked, streaky, striking, strong, subdued, subtle, sunny, swirling

<u>T</u>
Tacky, tinged, tinted, tonal, toned, traditional, translucent, transparent

<u>U</u>
Undiluted, uneven, uniform

<u>V</u>
Vibrant, vivid

<u>W</u>
Wan, warm, washed-out, waxen, wild

Enhance multicolored objects with adjectives such as these.

<u>B</u>
Bicolor, blended, braided

<u>C</u>
Cataclysmic-colored, checkered, compound, contrasting, crisscrossed

<u>D</u>
Dappled, disparate, dotted, dusted

<u>F</u>
Flecked, freckled, fused

<u>I</u>
Intermixed, interwoven

<u>J</u>
Jumbled

<u>L</u>
Lined

<u>K</u>
Kaleidoscopic

<u>M</u>
Many-hued, marbled, mingled, mixed, motley, mottled, multicolored, multihued

<u>P</u>
Particolored, patterned, peppered, piebald, pied, polychromatic, prismatic, psychedelic

<u>S</u>
Salted, speckled, splotched, stippled

<u>T</u>
Two-tone, tricolor

<u>V</u>
Varied, variegated, veined

Nouns provide more opportunities to add color and detail.

<u>A</u>
Accent

<u>B</u>
Bleach, brightness, brilliance

C
Chroma, clarity, CMYK, coating, color wheel, colorant, coloration, composite, cover

D
Deposit, depth, diffusion, dimension, dispersion, dye

F
Film, finish, flicker, fluorescence

G
Glare, glaze, gleam, glimmer, glint, glisten, glitter, glow, gradation

H
Henna, highlight, hint, hodgepodge, hue

I
Incandescence, intensity, iridescence

L
Lacquer, layer, lightness, lowlight, luminosity, luster

M
Mixture, moiré, monotone

N
Nuance

O
Opacity, opalescence

P
Paint, paisley, pantone, patchwork, patina, peroxide, pigment, pigmentation, plaid, polish, prism, purity

R
Radiance, rainbow, RGB, residue, rinse

S
Sample, saturation, seam, shade, sheen, shimmer, shine, smidgeon, sparkle, spectrum, stain, stratum, streak, stripe, suggestion, surface, swatch

T
Tartan, tattoo, tester, tier, tincture, tinge, tint, tone, touch, trace, twinkle

U
Undertone

V
Varnish, vein, veneer

Perhaps these verbs will provide inspiration.

Colors can blend, clash, or enhance. They might revitalize, fade, or overlap. Choose carefully to provide the nuance you need in your writing.

A
Accent, accentuate, appear, attract

B
Balance, bathe, bespatter, blanch, blare, blaze, blench, bleach, blend, blotch, brighten, brush, burn

C
Captivate, clash, color, combine, complement, conflict, contrast, coordinate, crayon

D
Darken, daub, draw, decolorize, decorate, deepen, dot, draw, dye

E
Embellish, emit, enhance, enliven

F
Fade, flare, flash, flatter, fleck

G
Glare, glaze, gleam, glimmer, glint, glisten, glow

H
Harmonize, heighten, highlight

I
Illuminate, infuse, intensify

J
Jar

L
Light, lighten

M
Match, meld, merge, mingle, mix

O
Outline, overlap

P
Paint, permeate, pervade, plaster

R
Radiate, revitalize

S
Saturate, seal, shade, shine, sketch, smear, sparkle, splash, splatter, spray, spread, stain, suffuse

T
Tinge, tint

V
Varnish

W
Wash

Invent colors.

Your ingenuity is the only limit with invented colors. Consider a few examples.

Yolanda sashayed toward me, hips swiveling in a seduction-red skirt that complemented her bad-baby-black lipstick.

Either Yolanda intends to ravish our narrator, or he hopes she's a bad girl with seduction on her mind.

Bruise-blue eyes stared out through glasses crisscrossed with cracks. Matching lumps burgeoned from Marco's chin and cheeks.

Readers will make the connection between *bruise-blue* and the lumps, imagining someone who has been beaten or injured.

Find color ideas by googling phrases such as "things that are green" or "things that look blue."

And now, a kaleidoscope of colors.

Some of the following lists contain invented colors. Many are based on objects we encounter in our environment. You can use almost any noun to create an adjective that will resonate with readers.

For the next several years, *Trump blond* or *Hillary blonde* will produce instant mental images.

Science fiction might use *deep-space black*, *quasar blue,* or *starburst yellow.*

An environmentalist could choose colors such as *oil-slick black, smog grey,* or *acid-rain yellow.*

Choose or invent colors that intensify your writing.

You can use many of these words as is, or precede the color they represent to produce a compound adjective. Rather than *anthracite*, for example, you might prefer *anthracite black.*

Black

Anger black, anthracite, bat black, boot black, cat black, cave black, cavity black, charcoal, coal black, crow black, deep-space black, ebony, evil black, funeral black, grease black, gunpowder black, ink, jade black, jet, leather black, licorice, metal black, midnight, mildew black, mold black, night black, obsidian, oil-slick black, onyx, pitch black, raven, sable, shadow black, shoe-polish black, silhouette black, smoky, sooty, spider black, spore black, stygian, tar black, tire black, tuxedo black, uber black, velvet black

Blond/Blonde

Although *blond* can be used for either males or females, I and many writers prefer *blond* to describe males and *blonde* to describe females. Likewise with gender-identified pets and animals.

Why?

Blond was adopted into English from French, and the French language uses gender-specific descriptors.

Compound adjectives in the following list are spelled with the feminine form.

Almond-crème blonde, albino blonde, amber, apple-cider blonde, apricot, ash blonde, banana-bread blonde, blanched, bleached, bombshell, bottle blonde, brassy, bronze, brown-sugar blonde, butter blonde, butternut, butterscotch, caramel, chamomile blonde, champagne, chardonnay blonde, corn blonde, diamond blonde, dirty blonde, dishwater blonde, electric blonde, flaxen, French-fry blonde, frosted blonde, gilded blonde, ginger, ginger-ale blonde, ginger spice, golden, goldenrod, Hillary blonde, honey blonde, honey-butter blonde, honeysuckle blonde, hot-toffee blonde, macadamia blonde, mushroom blonde, neon blonde, peroxide blonde, platinum, sand blonde, straw blonde, strawberry blonde, sunflower blonde, sun-kissed blonde, sunset blonde, tarnished-gold blonde, Trump blond/e, trumpet blonde, vanilla-malt blonde, vintage gold, wheat blonde

Blue

Admiral blue, Aegean blue, agate blue, arctic blue, azure, baby blue, berry blue, blue-jay blue, blue-jeans blue, bluebell blue, blueberry blue, blueberry-juice blue, bluebird blue, blue-jay blue, brook blue, bruise blue, cadet blue, Caribbean blue, cerulean, china-blue, cobalt, cornflower blue, crystal blue, denim blue, electric blue, forget-me-not blue, frostbite blue, galaxy blue, gunmetal blue, ice blue, indigo, ink blue, jellyfish blue, lagoon blue, lake blue, lapis blue, laser blue, lilac blue, lobelia blue, mold blue, moon blue, navy, ocean blue, quasar blue, river blue, robin-egg blue, sapphire blue, sky blue, star blue, steel blue, swimming-pool blue, teal, toilet-water blue, toothpaste blue, ultramarine

Brown

Acorn brown, almond brown, amber, auburn, autumn brown, Bambi brown, beige, brandy brown, brick brown, bronze, brunet, buckeye brown, camel brown, caramel, carob brown, cedar brown, champagne brown, chestnut, chipmunk brown, chocolate brown, cinnamon, cider brown, clay brown, coffee brown, cognac brown, cookie brown, copper, cork brown, desert sand, drab brown, dun brown, ecru, espresso brown, fawn brown, football brown, freckle brown, ginger, gingerbread brown, golden brown, hazel, hickory brown, honey brown, infrabeige, kiwi brown, lion brown, loam brown, mahogany, maroon, merlot brown, mocha, mouse brown, mud brown, muddy brown, nut brown, oak brown, October brown, orange brown, pancake brown, peanut brown, pecan brown, pekoe brown, penny brown, pigskin brown, pretzel brown, redwood, rosewood, russet, rust, sandstone brown, seal brown, sepia, sienna, slush brown, spice brown, syrup brown, taffy, tan, taupe, tawny brown, teak, teddy-bear brown, topaz brown, tortilla brown, tourmaline brown, umber, walnut, wheat brown, whiskey brown, wood brown

Green

Apple green, army green, artichoke green, asparagus green, avocado green, barf green, basil green, blue green, bottle green, bright green, cabbage green, camouflage green, cat's-eye green, celery green, chartreuse, clover green, crocodile green, crystal-marble green, cyan, electric green, elf green, emerald, fern green, fir green, frog green, Granny-Smith green, grape green, grass green, hypergreen, jade, jasper green, jelly green, juniper, kale green, khaki green, kiwi green, leaf green, LED green, olive, leprechaun green, lettuce green, lime, lizard green, loden, mildew green, mint, moss green, mucus green, neon green, ocean green, parsley green, pea green, pea-soup green, peacock green, pear green, Perrier-bottle green, pickle green, pine green, puke green, sage, sea green, seafoam green, seasick green, seaweed green, seedling green, shamrock green, snot green, spinach green, spring green, sprout green, spruce green, tea green, teal, toad green, velvet green, verdigris, viridian, watermelon green, yellow green

Grey/Gray

Alien grey, aluminum grey, anchor grey, ash grey, bad-news grey, battleship grey, bottle grey, boulder grey, carbon grey, cement grey, charcoal grey, cloud grey, coin grey, corpse grey, crater grey, death grey, dove grey, elephant grey, exhaust grey, fling grey, flint grey, fog grey, fossil grey, fungus grey, ginger grey, granite grey, graphite, gravel grey, gruel grey, gum grey, gunmetal grey, haze grey, hippo grey, hoary grey, ice grey, iron grey, knife grey, lead grey, mercury grey, meteor grey, mummy grey, nail grey, nickel, otter grey, pebble grey, pepper grey, pewter, pigeon grey, platinum grey, porpoise grey, porridge grey, rat grey, salt-and-pepper, seal grey, shadow grey, shark grey, shovel grey, silver, slate, sleet grey, slug grey, slush grey, smog grey, smoke, steel grey, stone grey, storm grey, stormy grey, stormy-sea grey, sword grey, tabby grey, tank grey, tweed grey, wax grey, wolf grey, zinc grey

Orange

Apricot orange, basketball orange, burnt orange, butternut orange, calypso orange, candlelight orange, cantaloupe orange, caramelized orange, carnelian, carotene orange, carrot orange, cayenne orange, cheddar orange, cheese-cracker orange, Chinese-lantern orange, cider orange, citrus orange, clementine orange, coral orange, crayon orange, curry orange, ember orange, fire orange, flame orange, goldfish orange, mac-and-cheese orange, mango-tango orange, mandarin orange, marigold orange, marmalade orange, monarch orange, nacho orange, nasturtium orange, naval orange, papaya orange, peach orange, peach-butter orange, peach-sorbet orange, popsicle orange, pumpkin orange, safety-vest orange, salamander orange, salmon orange, sherbet orange, shrimp orange, starfish orange, sunset orange, sweet-potato orange, tangelo orange, tangerine orange, terra cotta, tiger orange, traffic orange, yam orange

Pink

Amaranth, azalea pink, baby pink, ballet-slipper pink, begonia pink, blush, bright pink, bubblegum pink, cantaloupe pink, carnation pink, cerise, champagne pink, cherry-blossom pink, cherry-rose pink, coral, cotton-candy pink, crepe pink, cupid pink, cyclamen pink, damask, eraser pink, flamingo pink, fuchsia, geranium pink, grapefruit pink, lemonade pink, magenta, mandarin pink, mango pink, melon pink, old-rose pink, oleander pink, parfait pink, pastel pink, peach, peach-blossom pink, peony pink, piggy pink, piglet pink, pomegranate pink, powder pink, prom pink, punch pink, raspberry-smoothie pink, rose, rosewood pink, rouge pink, salmon pink, seashell pink, sherbet pink, shocking pink, strawberry pink, swine pink, taffy pink, watermelon pink, Zinfandel pink

Purple
Amethyst purple, amparo purple, aubergine, boysenberry purple, burgundy purple, Byzantium purple, claret purple, clover purple, concord purple, coneflower purple, cyclamen purple, eggplant purple, fandango purple, fig purple, gentian purple, gooseberry purple, grape purple, heather, heliotrope, hyacinth purple, indigo, iris purple, jam purple, kazoo purple, lavender, lilac, lollipop purple, lotus purple, magenta, mauve, mulberry purple, onion purple, opal purple, orchid purple, pansy purple, periwinkle purple, petunia purple, pillow purple, plum, posy purple, primrose purple, raisin purple, regalia purple, rhubarb purple, royal purple, sage-flower purple, sangria purple, sugar-plum purple, tanzanite purple, Tyrian purple, violet, wild-berry purple, wine purple, wisteria purple

Red
Alizarin crimson, apple red, auburn, beet red, berry red, blaze red, blood red, blush red, brick red, burgundy red, candy red, candy-apple red, candy-cane red, carrot red, cherry red, cherry-soda red, Christmas red, cinnabar, cinnamon-candy red, communist red, copper red, coral red, crab-apple red, cranberry red, crimson, currant red, devil red, fire red, fire-engine red, fire-hydrant red, flame red, flaming red, garnet red, ginger red, heart red, henna, holly-berry red, jam red, ketchup red, lady-bug red, LED red, licorice red, lipstick red, lobster red, maple-leaf red, merlot red, mulberry red, neon red, paprika, pepper red, pomegranate red, poppy red, radish red, raspberry red, roan, rose, rouge, ruby, Russian red, rust, rusty, Santa-suit red, scarlet, sorrel, stoplight red, strawberry red, sunburn red, titian, tomato red, tulip red, Valentine red, wanton red, watermelon red, wine red

White
Alabaster, albino white, angel white, ash white, birch white, blizzard white, bone white, bread-dough white, cake white, cameo white, chalk, chaste white, chiffon white, china white, clamshell white, cloud white, coconut white, cornstarch white, cream, crème, dandruff white, dumpling white, eggshell white, enamel white, fizz white, foam white, fog white, frost white, gardenia white, ghost white, goose-down white, heron white, hospital white, KKK white, ivory, lace white, lather white, lily white, linen white, lotus white, maggot white, milk white, mist white, moonstone white, mother-of-pearl white, noodle white, paper white, parchment white, pearl white, phantom white, picket white, platinum white, polar white, porcelain white, powder white, rice white, salt white, Samoyed white, sheet white, skeleton white, snowflake white, specter white, starch white, sugar white, talc white, vellum white, virgin white, wedding-veil white, winter white, wonton white

Yellow
Acid-rain yellow, autumn yellow, banana yellow, bourbon yellow, bumblebee yellow, butter yellow, buttercup yellow, butterfly yellow, butterscotch yellow, cadmium, canary yellow, chick yellow, citrine yellow, corn yellow, custard yellow, daffodil yellow, daisy yellow, dandelion yellow, Dijon yellow, duckling yellow, egg-yolk yellow, flaxen, ginger yellow, gold, goldenrod, grapefruit yellow, hardhat yellow, highlighter yellow, honey yellow, jaundice yellow, lemon, macaroni yellow, maize, mustard, omelet yellow, pencil yellow, pineapple yellow, plantain yellow, poppy yellow, rubber-ducky yellow, saffron, sallow yellow, sap yellow, sawdust yellow, school-bus yellow, scrambled-egg yellow, starburst yellow, sticky-note yellow, straw yellow, sulfur yellow, sun yellow, sunflower yellow, sweetcorn yellow, tallow yellow, taxi yellow, turmeric yellow, wasp yellow, whisky yellow, yield-sign yellow

Smell: Scent Words

Why should you incorporate scent in your prose or poetry?

Our brains associate scent with memories. The whiff of an orchid might remind a woman of her senior prom, reawakening visceral recollections of music, embarrassment over a zipper that popped open at an inopportune moment, or the adrenaline rush of a passionate kiss behind the bleachers.

A pine freshener hanging from the rearview mirror of a taxi could flood a passenger with memories of a drive into the desert to ditch the corpse of an ex-lover. The memories might be so strong that he wets his pants or hears the non-existent screams of his dying victim.

Use scent to your advantage. Spritz aroma throughout your writing, as you might air freshener in a stale room, to stimulate readers' olfactory centers.

Alternative nouns for *scent*.

The word *aroma* conveys an impression of something pleasant, whereas *smell* could refer to unpleasant scents. Choose carefully. The difference between *fragrance* and *stench* can reverse the undertone of a passage.

Select a word that suits the situation:

Aroma, attar, aura, balm, bouquet, distillate, essence, fragrance, hint, perfume, pong, redolence, reek, smell, spoor, stench, stink, suggestion, tang, tinge, trace, trail, undertone, waft, whiff, whisper

What produced the smell?

Study a few examples.

Her hair smelled like bubblegum mixed with cotton candy.

A coppery stench oozed from the wound.

His bacon breath turned her stomach.

Why would bacon turn someone's stomach? Story prompt?

The air was laced with smells that spoke of [Insert an appropriate noun.]

The following *Pleasant* and *Unpleasant* lists contain words you could include in direct comparisons. Transform nouns into adjectives by adding appropriate suffixes, or, if appropriate, insert as is. What seems pleasant to you could nauseate your protagonist, so you might want to switch some of the words.

Pleasant
Air-dried sheets, angels' breath, anise, baby powder, baby's breath, bacon, fresh-baked bread, bananas, bubblegum, cedar, chamomile, chicken broth, chocolate, cinnamon, citrus, cocoa, coconut, coffee, cork, cotton candy, eucalyptus, flowers, forest, fresh air, fruit, Grandma's kitchen, grass, hand cream, hand sanitizer, honey, leather, lemon, licorice, lilacs, lime, lipstick, maple sugar, meadow, mint, ocean breeze, oranges, peaches, pine, pineapple, pizzeria, popcorn, roses, scented soap, strawberries, summer day, toast, vanilla, violets, wine, woods/forest, yeast

Unpleasant
Acetone, bad breath, barbeque, barnyard, bat guano, burning lint, burning oil, burning tire, camel breath, cat box, cemetery, chicken coop, chlorine, cigars, cleaning fluid, copper, corpse, decomp, dog, dog breath, fish, fresh blood, fresh paint, funky fungus, garbage dump, garlic, gas pump, greasy rags, green bacon, hair dye, hospital, hot tar, kitty-litter, laundry hamper, locker room, medicine, metal, mildew, mold, moldy dentures, musty attic, nail polish, nicotine, onions, pepper, plastic, rancid butter/cheese, ripe socks, rotten potatoes, rotting whale carcass, saddle, scorched rubber, seaweed, sewer, skunk, smoke, stringent soap, sulfur, sweat, tobacco, toe jams, tuna, vinegar, well-used sheets

Describe scents with well-chosen adjectives.

If you're writing a horror novel, you can create a feeling of suspense by foreshadowing. Contrast and compare. Maybe your monster has a delicate woodsy aroma that lures its victims deep into a musty lair where it dissolves the flesh from their bones with a caustic venom that reeks of corpses and singed hair.

Make a romance steamier by including adjectives such as *sweaty, masculine, intoxicating,* and *spicy.*

A
Acetic, acid, acrid, airy, alluring, ambrosial, antiseptic, aromatic

B
Balmy, bitter, biting, bland, briny, burnt

C
Caustic, clean, clear, comforting, cool, crisp, cutting

D
Damp, dank, decaying, decomposing, delicate, dirty, discreet, distinctive

E
Earthy, elusive, enticing, exhilarating

F
Faint, feminine, fetid, fishy, floral, flowery, forceful, foul, fragrant, fresh, fusty

G
Gamey, gaseous, gentle, giddy

H
Heady, hearty, heavy, honeyed

I
Intoxicating, invigorating, irresistible

L
Light, loamy, low-key

M
Malodorous, masculine, mild, moist, musky, musty

N
Nauseating, new

<u>O</u>
Odorous, overpowering

<u>P</u>
Perfumed, piquant, pleasant, polluted, potent, pungent, putrescent, putrid

<u>R</u>
Rancid, rank, redolent, refined, refreshing, repulsive, rich, ripe, rotten

<u>S</u>
Savory, seductive, sharp, sickly, smelly, sour, spicy, spoiled, squalid, stagnant, stale, sterile, stinking, strong, stuffy, subtle, sweaty, sweet, syrupy

<u>T</u>
Tainted, tangy, tantalizing, tart, tempting, thrilling

<u>U</u>
Unassuming, unclean, understated, uninteresting

<u>W</u>
Wholesome

Here are few objects and places that will help incorporate scent in your writing:

Airport waiting areas, antique stores, breath, clothing, delicatessens, elevators, feet, flea markets, food, hair, hands, libraries, money, old books, parades, pets, plants, public transit, seating places, vehicles, weather, wooden objects

Wax creative.

He stank like a conservative, she like a liberal.

He reeked of desperation.

The storm swept in with a roiling stench of fresh blood and burning bodies.

Agonizing odors smothered the battlefield, emanating unfulfilled dreams and fresh blood.

Something could have no smell at all:

Flat, fragrance-free, inodorous, neutral, odor-free, odorless, scentless, unscented

Lack of scent can create suspense.

The tracker sniffed the footprints. Why could he detect nothing but moss and pine and fear? Only a moon-gloxx could leave such spoor.

Tabitha's translucent form shifted and hovered above the bed, bereft of substance and scent.

Give scent a try. You'll be glad you did.

Taste Words

"Nothing takes the taste out of peanut butter quite like unrequited love." ~ Charles M. Schulz in the persona of Charlie Brown

Why should you incorporate taste in your writing?

Your prose or poetry doesn't have to be *tasteful*, but the best creative works include the *sense of taste*.

Charles M. Schulz understood that and turned it upside down to make a point.

Taste is one of the most important senses. We might wake in the morning with a putrid flavor in our mouth. Our first urge is to rinse with mouthwash or drink a cup of coffee.

We celebrate special occasions with food. We're always on the hunt for that extraordinary entrée with just the right combination of seasonings.

We recoil when something is too spicy, sour, or overcooked. We might forgive a restaurant for slow service, but not for a dish that doesn't please our palate.

Add taste to your writing, and it will sizzle with new life.

How can you include taste?

Besides the obvious, adding it with food, consider describing the tastes of other objects in your story's environment. Here are a few to stimulate your creativity.

- Blood from a split lip.

- Chemicals in swimming pool water, gulped during a long swim or near-drowning.

- Coins a character in a period piece might bite on to see if they're real.

- Grass or doggy-doo weed-whipped into the face.

- Ink from a pen that a nerd chews while thinking.

- Mud or rocks a child stuffs into the mouth while playing or pretending.

- Sweat trickling onto the lips during vigorous exercise or a high-speed chase.

- Water dripping off a frozen beard or mustache.

- Puzzle pieces crammed into a child's mouth.

A few more:

Baby soother, bile, chewing gum, chewing tobacco, cigars/cigarettes, dandelion fluff, dental packing, dental procedures, dentures, fingernails, fingers, hair, heartburn, lipstick, medication, mints, mud, ocean spray, phlegm, pipe tobacco, play dough, rain, runny nose, shampoo, skin, smoke, snow, soap, stole/boa/scarf, toothpaste, turtleneck, wind

Taste doesn't function in a vacuum.

Have you noticed that when your noise is plugged, your food tastes different? Taste and scent are connected. In fact, experts say these senses are our body's way of identifying and interacting with the myriad of chemicals in our world. If you taste something you can often smell it, and vice versa. Likewise with texture.

Therefore, some of the following words could refer to scent or texture too. Embrace these senses as well to produce the most vivid prose and poetry.

Taste **adjectives.**

A
Acerbic, acidic, acrid, aged, alkaline, ambrosial, appetizing, astringent

B
Barny, basic, benign, biting, bitter, bittersweet, bland, blissful, blistering, bloody, blubbery, boring, bracing, brackish, briny, brisk, bubbly, buttery, burnt, buttery

C

Caramel, cardboard, carbonated, caustic, celestial, chalky, charcoal, charred, cheesy, chewy, chocolatey, cinnamon, citrus, citrusy, clove-like, coarse, comforting, complex, concentrated, cool, coppery, corrosive, creamy, crisp, crumbly, curdled, curious, cutting

D

Delectable, delicate, delicious, delightful, delish, desiccated, distinct, divine, dreary, dry, dull, dusty

E

Earthy, effervescent, eggy, elastic, elusive, enjoyable, exquisite

F

Faint, fatty, fermented, fibrous, fiery, filling, fishy, fizzy, flakey, flat, flavorful, flavorless, flavorsome, flowery, floury, foamy, foul, fresh, fried, frosty, frothy, fruity, full, full-bodied, fusty

G

Gamey, garlicky, gentle, ghastly, gingery, glacial, grainy, granular, grapey, grassy, gratifying, gravelly, greasy, green, gristly, gritty, grungy

H

Hard-to-chew, harsh, heady, healthy, hearty, heavenly, heavy, herbal, herbed, herby, honey, honeyed, hork-inducing, horsey, hot, humdrum

I

Icy, immature, indistinct, inedible, insipid, intense, invigorating

J

Juicy

K

Keen

L

Leathery, lemony, light, limey, lip-smacking, lively, luscious

M

Malty, marinated, mature, medicinal, mellow, metallic, mild, mildewy, milky, minty, moist, moldy, monotonous, mouthwatering, muddy, mulled, multi-layered, mushy, musty, muted, mysterious

N

Nippy, nutty

O

Obscure, odd, off, oily, oniony, overcooked, overdone, overpowering

P

Palatable, passable, pasty, peanutty, peculiar, pedestrian, peppery, perfect, perky, pickled, piquant, plain, pleasant, pleasing, plummy, polluted, potent, powdery, powerful, pungent

Q

Quenching

R

Rancid, rare, red-hot, refined, refreshing, revitalizing, rich, ripe, robust, rotten, rough, rubbery

S

Salty, sandy, satiating, sating, satisfying, savory, scalding, scorched, scrummy, scrumptious, searing, seasoned, sharp, sinewy, skunky, slaking, slick, slight, slimy, smoky, smooth, soapy, sodden, soggy, sooty, sophisticated, sour, sparkling, spiced, spicy, spoiled, spongy, squidgy, squishy, stale, starchy, sterile, strange, strident, stringy, strong, subdued, subtle, succulent, sudsy, sugary, sulfurous, superb, sweet, sweet-and-sour, syrupy

T

Tainted, tangy, tantalizing, tart, tasteless, tasty, tedious, tender, thick, thirst-quenching, tinny, titillating, toasty, toothsome, torrid, tough

U

Unappetizing, undercooked, underdone, under-ripe, unexciting, unflavored, uninteresting, unpalatable, unpleasant, unpretentious, unseasoned, unsalted, unsophisticated

V
Vague, vanilla, velvety, vinegary, viscous, vivid

W
Winey, waterlogged, watery, weak, well-done, wintry, wishy-washy, woody

Y
Yeasty, yucky, yummy

Z
Zesty, zingy

Touch: Temperature Words

Temperature embodies more than heat and cold.

Applied effectively in prose or poetry, heat or lack of it can express subtleties of emotion, hence terms such as *hot-tempered* and *cold-hearted*.

Ambient temperature affects sleep patterns, productivity, and emotions.

Excessive heat irritates tempers. Your characters might quarrel without realizing they're responding to the environment. Or your protagonists could blame their bad mood, blushing, or sweating on temperature while hiding the true reasons for their behavior.

Cold surroundings can draw people together to share body heat. Men have exploited this fact for centuries to entice women into their arms.

Temperature may indicate good or ill health, pleasant or unpleasant weather, good or bad omens.

People expect certain types of food, such as soup, to be hot. Serve a guest cold gazpacho, and you might expect a surprised reaction.

Hot liquids stain more readily than their cold counterparts. Story fodder? Perhaps your protagonist deliberately spills hot coffee into someone's lap to spur the removal of pants or skirt.

Young women who are not ready to get pregnant sometimes have their eggs frozen in order to bear children later in life. What would happen if one of these women met a sperm donor at a reproduction clinic and they started dating?

Although today's technology can't reanimate corpses, some people choose to have their bodies vitrified and cryogenically preserved after death in hopes that future scientists will be able to revive them.

A chase through the hot desert will require different props and plotlines than a similar event at the South Pole.

Heat sterilizes objects and food. Freezing doesn't. That's why frozen corpses of animals and humans can pose a risk to modern generations: they harbor microorganisms that could be dangerous to a non-immune population.

Someone trying to save money might turn the heat down in the winter; likewise with air conditioning during summer months. This might cause complications with health, pets, and houseplants.

Incinerators burn confidential documents. *"Oops! I swear, boss, Findlay tripped when he was disposing of the top-secret files. The burns on my hands? I ... uh ... tried to rescue him. Yeah, that's it. I tried to rescue him."*

Story prompts ahead.

Some of the preceding paragraphs may have given you ideas for stories or plot twists. Please enjoy a few more.

1. A patient's temperature reads several degrees lower than usual.

2. Wife repeatedly turns the heat down. Husband turns it back up.

3. Thirteen months of stifling summer weather stumps scientists.

4. Bears decide to hibernate three months early.

5. A three-acre patch of ice forms in the Bay of Bengal.

6. A pendant grows warm whenever anyone nearby tells a lie.

7. A talking refrigerator develops a personality.

Words, words, and more words await your review.

The following lists contain over 400 words that will help you include temperature in your writing.

Hot **adjectives.**

A
Ablaze, afire, aflame, Africa-hot, asmolder, autoclaving

B
Baking, blackening, blazing, blistering, boiling, branding, broiling, browned, burning

C
Charring, close

D
Deep-fried, extreme

F
Febrile, fevered, feverish, feverous, fiery, flaming, frying

H
Hyper-heated, hyper-hot, hyperthermic

I
Intense

M
Melting, molten, muggy

N
Nuclear

O
Oppressive, overheated

P
Parching, piping, poker-hot

R
Red-hot, roasting

S
Sanitizing, sautéing, scalding, scorching, searing, shriveling, singeing, sizzling, smoking, smoldering, steaming, sterilizing, sticky, stifling, sultry, sweaty, sweltering

T
Thermonuclear, torrid, tropical

<u>W</u>
Wilting, withering

***Hot* nouns.**

<u>A</u>
Ash, asphalt

<u>B</u>
Barbecue, blast furnace, blaze, boiling point, bonfire, branding iron, burner (of a stove), burning tires

<u>C</u>
Candle flame, car hood, cattle prod, clinker, coals, coffee, conflagration, cooking oil, curling iron

<u>D</u>
Deep fryer, demon's tears, desert, dragon's breath

<u>E</u>
Ember, equator, exhaust manifold/pipe, exploding meteor

<u>F</u>
Fever, fire, firecracker, fireplace, fireworks, flashpoint, floodlights, forge, French fries, frying pan, fryolator, furnace

<u>G</u>
Geyser, glue gun, griddle, grill

<u>H</u>
Hades, heartburn, heat lamp, Hell, hot springs, hot tar

<u>I</u>
Incalescence, incinerator, infected wound, inferno, iron

<u>K</u>
Kiln

<u>L</u>
Lightbulb, lightning

276

M
Magma, melting point, mineral spring, molten lava, molten metal, molten wax

O
Oast, oven

P
Pavement

R
Radiator, rocket, rocket exhaust

S
Sahara, sidewalk, slag, solar flare, soldering iron, soup, stage lights, steam bath, stove burner, summer sun, sunburn, sunspot, supernova

T
Tin roof

V
Volcano

W
Wildfire, wok

Hot verbs.

A
Arc, autoclave

B
Bake, barbecue, blaze, blister, boil, braise, brand, broil, brown, bubble, burn, burst into flames

C
Carbonize, catch fire, cauterize, char, commit arson, cook, cremate

D
Deep-fry, defrost, detonate, disinfect

E
Explode

F
Fan the flames, fire, flame, flare, flash, fry, fuel

G
Glow, go off, go up in flames, grill

H
Heat

I
Ignite, immolate, incinerate

K
Kindle

L
Light, liquefy

M
Melt, microwave

N
Nuke

O
Overcook, overheat

P
Pan-fry, parboil, perspire, poach

R
Reduce to ashes, refry, reheat, rewarm, roast

S
Sanitize, sauté, scald, scorch, scramble, sear, set a match to, set alight, simmer, singe, smolder, solder, spark, steam, steam-clean, sterilize, stew, stir-fry, strike a match, sweat, swelter

<u>T</u>
Thaw, toast, torch

<u>W</u>
Warm

<u>Z</u>
Zap

Warm adjectives.

<u>A</u>
Agreeable

<u>B</u>
Balmy, blood-warm

<u>C</u>
Clement, comfortable, comfy, cozy

<u>E</u>
Enjoyable

<u>F</u>
Fair, fine

<u>H</u>
Homey

<u>I</u>
Inviting

<u>L</u>
Lukewarm

<u>M</u>
Mellow, mild, moderate

<u>P</u>
Pleasant

<u>R</u>
Restful, room-temperature

<u>S</u>
Slightly warm, snug, summery

<u>T</u>
Temperate, tepid, toasty

<u>W</u>
Warm, warmish

***Warm* nouns.**

<u>A</u>
Armpits

<u>B</u>
Baby toes, baby's breath, baby's laugh, baby's smile, bathwater, blood, breath, buns

<u>C</u>
Chick, clothes from the dryer, cow manure

<u>D</u>
Dog/cat doo-doo, dog/cat vomit

<u>E</u>
Ear muffs, embrace

<u>F</u>
Flannel, freshly baked bread/buns, freshly laid egg

<u>G</u>
Gloves, groin

<u>H</u>
Hand warmers, handshake, happy book/movie

<u>J</u>
Just-vacated seat

<u>K</u>
Kiss, kitten

<u>L</u>
Lover's body/smile

<u>M</u>
Memory foam, milk before bed, mitts, mother's smile

<u>P</u>
Parka, pee, puppy

<u>R</u>
Rope/rug burn

<u>S</u>
Spit, sunshine, sweater

<u>T</u>
Tongue

<u>W</u>
Welcome, wool socks

Warm verbs.

Empty list. If something is cold, you require a hot verb to warm it; if it's hot, you need a cold verb to bring it to a warm state.

Cold adjectives.

<u>A</u>
Algid, Antarctic, Arctic, austere

<u>B</u>
Benumbed, biting, bitter, bitterly cold, bleak, bone-chilling, bracing, brisk, brumal

<u>C</u>
Chilly, congealed, cool, crisp, cryogenic

<u>D</u>
Desolate, drafty, dreary

<u>E</u>
Exhilarating, extreme

<u>F</u>
Freezing, fresh, frigid, frigorific, frore, frosty, frozen

<u>G</u>
Gelid, glacial

<u>H</u>
Harsh, hibernal, hiemal, hoary, hypothermic

<u>I</u>
Icebound, icebox, ice-capped, ice-cold, ice-kissed, icicled, icy, icy-cold, intense, invigorating

<u>K</u>
Keen

<u>N</u>
Nippy, numbed, numbing

<u>P</u>
Penetrating, piercing, polar

<u>R</u>
Raw, refrigerated, rimy

<u>S</u>
Severe, sharp, shivery, Siberian, sleety, snappy, snowy, stimulating, stinging, subzero

<u>W</u>
Wintry

***Cold* nouns.**

<u>A</u>
Abominable Snowman, absolute zero, Alaska, avalanche

<u>B</u>
Banana split, Bigfoot, blizzard, brain freeze

<u>C</u>
Cemetery, condenser fins, crushed ice, cryobank, cryobiologist, cryodesiccation, cryoscope, cryostat, cryosurgery, cryotherapy

<u>D</u>
Dark side of the moon, deep sea, dry ice

<u>E</u>
Evaporator coils, ex's feet, ex's heart/scorn

<u>F</u>
Father's criticism, freezer, freezing point, frostbite, frozen fish, Fudgesicle

<u>G</u>
Glacier

<u>H</u>
Hoarfrost

<u>I</u>
Ice chest, ice cube, iceberg, ice-cream cone, igloo

<u>L</u>
Liquid nitrogen

<u>M</u>
Milk shake, Mount Everest

<u>N</u>
North Pole

<u>O</u>
Ocean trench

<u>P</u>
Penguin, plutonian crater/mountain, polar bear, popsicle

<u>R</u>
Reykjavik

<u>S</u>
Sherbet, shoulder, Siberia, skating rink, ski hill, sled dog, slushy, snow angel, snowbank, snowflake, snowman, South Pole

<u>W</u>
Wind, wind chill, winter, witch's toe

<u>Y</u>
Yeti

Cold **verbs.**

<u>A</u>
Air-condition

<u>B</u>
Bite

<u>C</u>
Chill, congeal, cool, crystalize

<u>D</u>
Deep-freeze

<u>F</u>
Flash-freeze, freeze, frost

<u>G</u>
Gel, glaciate

<u>H</u>
Harden

I
Ice, ice-over, ice-up, infrigidate

J
Jell

K
Keep cold

L
Lose heat, lower the temperature

P
Preserve, put on ice

R
Refrigerate, rime

S
Set, solidify, sting

T
Turn to ice

V
Vitrify

Other adjectives.

A
Abnormal, above-zero, absolute, adiabatic, air, ambient, annual, atmospheric, average, axillary (armpit)

B
Basal, below-zero, body

C
Calescent, Celsius, critical

D
Daily, daytime, decalescent, diurnal

E
Elevated, environmental, external, extreme

F
Fahrenheit, favorable, fixed

G
Global

H
High

I
Ideal, indoor, inside, internal

K
Kelvin

L
Low

M
Maximum, mean, metabolic, minimum, minus, moderate, monthly

O
Ocean, optimum, oral (mouth), outdoor, outside, oven, overall

P
Peak, plus, preferred

R
Raised, recalescent, recommended, recorded, rectal, reduced, regulated, relative, requisite, room

S
Seasonal, soil, stable, standard, static, subnormal, substrate, surface

T
Temporal (forehead), thermodynamic, thermogenic, thermostatic, tympanic (ear), typical

<u>U</u>
Underground, uniform

<u>V</u>
Volatile

<u>W</u>
Water

<u>Y</u>
Yearly

Other nouns.

Homeostasis, isotherm, lyophilization, thermocline, thermocouple, thermogram, thermometer, thermoreceptor, thermoregulator, thermos, thermostat, vital signs

Touch: Texture Words

Engage the senses, and you engage readers.

Visuals are often a writer's first consideration. We might describe dimensions, shape, and color. Sound could come next, followed by scent. We might assign taste attributes to food, teardrops, and lipstick.

Sadly, many writers undervalue texture.

After reading this paragraph, close your eyes and imagine a piece of driftwood that has been sitting on a shelf for three years. How would you describe it? Take your time.

...

Consider the following. After three years, the wood releases no scent. It lies on the shelf, silent. If you decide to check its taste, your tongue might pick up dust, or maybe it would catch on a knobby protuberance.

Using your sense of touch, your fingers would feel grain or grooves; you'd notice hardness and temperature.

A few well-chosen texture words can add depth and intrigue.

Clanton's palms patted the surface on both sides of her body. They were met with the velvety texture of ... moss? It certainly wasn't the carpeting in her office.

Three sentences. Two texture words. We intuit that Clanton is confused, and we can assume she's in a forest. Or is she?

Jens rubbed the threadbare tweed sleeve of his jacket. Although his hand hitched over the knife strapped beneath, he hoped no one would notice his keen messenger of justice.

Why is Jens wearing a threadbare jacket? To whom will he administer justice, and why? *Keen* could apply to his fervor as well as the sharpness of the knife.

Vary your style occasionally to lead with texture.

Do you always describe how something looks and then follow with everything else?

Why?

Whenever you write descriptions, imagine how a blind person perceives the world. A well-chosen texture adjective will invigorate your words.

Everything touchable has texture. Pick up a tin-can lid, a paper towel, or a cutting board. Each has a unique surface, distinguishable with closed eyes.

Smooth describes texture, but smooth objects have distinct surfaces. Consider the variations between a tin can, a plastic jar, and a water glass. All three could be described as smooth, but your fingers will discern the difference.

Instead of *smooth*, consider:

Tinny, plastic, glassy
Metallic, flexible, glossy
Rusty, slick, glazed

Each adjective carries a different connotation.

The body senses texture in multiple ways.

Feet will feel the wooden slats of a swaying footbridge, the give of snowshoes in fluffy snow, or the chafing of a rock in the shoe.

The entire body will sense vibrations when a vehicle shimmies across the steel deck of a bridge.

Pine needles on the forest floor might lodge in socks and pants, causing prickly tingles.

Burrs will stick to clothing and hair, irritating wherever they touch skin.

Tongues are adept at analyzing food textures and detecting goosebumps on a lover's neck.

Speaking of lovers, have you ever worn silk underwear or slept in satin sheets? How would you describe the experience?

Consider these avenues for adding texture.

Warning: You might find a few story prompts and plot twists in the following list.

- Knees grating over gravel, splintered boards, or desiccated bones.

- Heels rubbing against ankle cuffs or rough ridges in shoes.

- Bare elbows contacting with people in a crowd or zombies on the prowl.

- Nose or buttocks reacting to cheap tissues or toilet paper.

- Chin chafing against a muzzle or rough wool scarf.

- Ears irritated by a scratchy hatband, collar, or blindfold.

- Cheeks bumpy after an overnight stint sleeping on the couch.

- Back aching because of a lumpy mattress or a long ride in a trunk.

- Wrists raw from rubbing against handcuffs or rope restraints.

- Thighs covered with red welts from stinging nettle.

- Legs brushing by a pet, bush, or hanging corpse.

- Fingernails broken after scouring dried blood from the floor.

- Fingers gooey from scraping bubblegum off a chandelier.

- Fingertips freezing while scratching frost off a car window.

- Lips brittle and split from days in the desert or at sea.

- Eyes gritty with debris dislodged by helicopter blades.

Texture surrounds us. It deserves a prominent place in your writing.

Do you have an inventive mind?

Shakespeare coined many words in common use. From his pen came adjectives such as *caked, gnarled,* and *lustrous.* You've probably used at least one of his words today.

Add *able, al, est, esque, free, ful, ible, ic, ish, ive, less, like, oid, ous,* and other suffixes to nouns and verbs to create new adjectives.

Let's consider *angora, asphalt,* and *concrete.* We're already familiar with their texture. *Angoraful* could describe a baby's hair. *Asphaltous* might be appropriate for whisker stubble. *Concretesque* would be an excellent description for a fitness trainer's abs.

Better yet, combine words. *Smog* is a combination of *smoke* and *fog. Brexit* was formed by joining *British* and *exit. Chortle* is a merging of *chuckle* and *snort.*

Your creativity is your only limit.

Ready for the *supercalifragilisticexpialidocious* list?

Supercalifragilisticexpialidocious is another invented adjective so well-known that it didn't trigger a warning from my spell checker.

The following table presents over 400 texture adjectives. Use them as is or try combining a few. How about *ticklehairy, bristlehatched,* or *gummysoft,* for example?

A
Abrasive, adhesive, alligator-like, armadillo, armored, asymmetrical

B
Bald, barbed, barnacled, bearded, bearskin, blanketed, blemished, blistered, bony, braided, brick, bristly, brittle, broken, bubbled, bubbly, buffed, bumpy, bunched, burnished, burred, bushy, buttery

C
Caked, calcified, cardboard-like, carved, cedar, chafed, chafing, chainmail, chalky, channeled, chaotic, chipped, chiseled, cleft, clotted, clumped, coagulated, coarse, cobbled, concave, concrete, congealed,

convex, corduroy, corky, corroded, corrugated, cottony, cracked, cracking, cratered, creamy, creased, crenelated, crepe-like, crimped, crinkled, crisp, crispy, crisscrossed, crocheted, crocodilian, crooked, crosshatched, crude, crumbly, crumpled, crushed, crusted, crusty, crystalline, curtained, cushioned, cushiony, cutting

D
Damaged, delicate, dense, dented, depressed, diaphanous, dinted, distorted, dotted, doughy, downy, drooping, ductile, dull

E
Earthen, edged, elastic, emblazoned, embossed, embroidered, emery, enameled, encrusted, engraved, entwined, ermine, erupted, etched, even

F
Feathery, felt, festered, fibrous, filamented, filigreed, filmy, fine, firm, fissured, flabby, flaccid, flaky, flat, flattened, flawed, flawless, fleecy, fleshy, flexible, flinty, flocculent, floppy, fluffy, fluted, foamy, folded, frayed, friable, frilled, frilly, frozen, furred, furrowed, furry, fuzzy

G
Gashed, gathered, gauzy, gelatinous, gelled, gilded, glassy, glazed, glossy, glutinous, gnarled, gnarly, gooey, gouged, grainy, granular, granulated, grating, gravelly, graven, greasy, gristly, gritty, grooved, gummy

H
Hacked, hairless, hairy, hard, hard-packed, harsh, hatched, hempen, hewn, hirsute, holey, honeycombed, hooked, horned

I
Ice-covered, impenetrable, imperfect, imprecise, imprinted, incised, incrusted, indented, inelastic, inflexible, inlaid, inscribed, inset, interlaced, interlocked, intertwined, interwoven, intricate, ironed, irregular, itchy

J
Jacquard-woven, jagged, jellied, jeweled, jumbled

K
Keen, knitted, knobbly, knobby, knotted, knotty

L
Laced, lacy, latticed, layered, leathern, leathery, level, limp, lined, linen, liquid, lizard-like, lumpy

M
Malleable, marked, marred, mashed, matte, matted, meshed, metallic, mirror-smooth, misshapen, molten, mortared, mosaic, mossy, mottled, mulchy, mushy, mutilated

N
Nappy, needled, needlelike, neoprene-covered, nicked, nodular, notched, nubby

O
Oily, ossified, overlaid

P
Padded, papery, parchment-thin, patched, patchy, patinated, patterned, paved, pebbled, pebbly, peeling, petrified, pigskin, pillowy, pinked, pitted, plaited, plastered, plastic, pleated, pliable, pliant, plumose, plumy, plush, pocked, pockmarked, pointed, polished, porous, potholed, powdery, pressed, prickly, printed, protuberant, puckered, puffy, pulpy

Q
Quilled, quilted

R
Ragged, rasped, razor-sharp, regular, reptilian, ribbed, rich, ridged, rigid, rocky, rough, roughspun, rubbery, rubbled, rucked, ruffled, rumpled, runneled, runny, rusty, rutted

S
Sable, sackcloth, sanded, sandpapery, sandy, satiny, scalloped, scaly, scarred, scooped, scored, scraped, scratched, scratchy, scrubby, scrunched, sculpted, sculptured, sealskin, seamed, serpentine, serrated, set-in, shaggy, sharp, sharp-edged, shaved, shingled, shirred, shorn, shredded, shriveled, silken, silky, slashed, slate, sleek,

slick, slimy, slippery, slit, slithery, smooth, snarled, soapy, soft, soggy, solid, spattered, speckled, spiked, spiny, splintered, split, spongy, springy, squashy, squidgy, squishy, stamped, steely, sticky, stiff, stitched, stony, straw-like, streaked, stretchy, stringy, stubbly, stuccoed, studded, stuffed, supple, suppurated, syrupy

T

Tacky, tapestried, tarnished, tattered, taut, tensile, terrycloth-draped, tessellated, thatched, thick, thin, thorny, threadbare, threadlike, tickling, tickly, tiled, tinny, tooled, toothed, toothy, torn, tough, tufted, tweedy, twilled, twisted

U

Unblemished, undulating, uneven, uniform, unshaven, unshorn, unyielding, upholstered

V

Varnished, veined, veinous, velveteen, velvety, veneered, viscid, viscous

W

Wadded, waffled, warped, washboard, watery, wattled, wavy, waxen, waxy, weather-beaten, webbed, well-defined, well-honed, whipped, whiskery, whorled, wilted, wiry, withered, wizened, wooden, woody, woolen, woolly, wormholed, worn, worsted, woven, wrinkled, wrought

Y

Yielding

The Environment

Conventional advice recommends that writers open with action. Starting a story with descriptions of weather and the environment contravenes that advice.

However, add the right mood with dripping water or whipping wind, and your writing will benefit. No purple prose needed—just a few well-placed words.

Water Words

The more senses you stimulate in your writing, the more you involve readers. Water provides an indirect way to accomplish that.

We all know what water feels like: wet. However, it can also feel cold, hot, or slimy. It can roil like an angry spirit, hiss as though it were a poisonous viper, or lie smooth and serene on a sunny day.

Along with weather, water can set a mood. The word suggestions in this chapter comprise three sections: *Adjectives, Verbs*, and *Nouns.* You can form verbs from many of the nouns and vice versa, or create adjectives by adding *ing* to many of the verbs.

Let's consider *burble*, used once as a noun, next as a verb, and finally as an adjective, in three simple sentences:

The <u>burble</u> of the brook woke her from a deep slumber.

The brook <u>burbled</u>, waking her from a deep slumber.

The <u>burbling</u> brook woke her from a deep slumber.

Now let's get more creative. Which of the following do you prefer?

The boys walked home from school. By the time they got there, their boots were all wet.

The boys meandered home from school, splooshing in every puddle they discovered, until their boots filled with muck.

The second example, just one word longer, paints a picture. Can you see the boys, covered with muddy water and soaked to the skin?

Drill through the lists and marinate with imagination to make your writing sparkle.

Adjectives

<u>A</u>
Abysmal, aerated, angry, aquatic, arctic, ashore

Bitter, blistering, bloated, bottomless, bracing, brackish, briny, bubbly

Calm, carbonated, chaotic, chilly, choppy, clamorous, clear, cloudy, coastal, coastward, cold, contaminated, cool, crossable, crystal-clear

Dangerous, deep, deep-sea, dirty, downriver, drizzly

Effervescent

Feral, fetid, filthy, fizzy, fluvial, foamy, foul, freezing, fresh, frothy

Glacial, glassy, gloomy

Hazardous, heavy, high, hostile, hot

Icy, inshore

Landward, littoral, low, lukewarm

Marine, maritime, menacing, mirror-like, moist, mucky, muddy, murky

Nautical, naval, navigable, noisy

Oceangoing, oceanic, offshore, ominous, opaque

Passable, peaceful, perilous, placid, polar, polluted, prismatic, pure

Q
Quiet

R
Rainy, reflective, refreshing, relaxing, rough

S
Saline, saltwater, salty, seafaring, seagoing, seaside, seaworthy, serene, shallow, shiny, showery, slick, slimy, sloppy, sluggish, smooth, sodden, soggy, squelchy, stagnant, still, stormy, sudsy, swollen

T
Tainted, temperate, tempestuous, tepid, thick, tidal, torpid, torrential, tranquil, tropical, turbulent, turgid

U
Undisturbed, untainted, untamed, upriver

V
Violent, viscous

W
Warm, waterlogged, wavy, wet, wholesome, wild, wintry

Verbs

B
Baptize, bathe, bedew, besprinkle, boil, break, buckle, burble, burst

C
Churn, clap, course, crash, creep, curve

D
Dabble, dampen, dilute, douse, drench, drill, drive, drown, drum, duck, dump, dunk

E
Ebb, engulf, erupt, explode, exude

F
Flush, freeze

G
Glitter, gurgle, gush

H
Heave, hiss, hose, humidify

I
Immerse, inch, irrigate

L
Lade, lap, launder, lave, leap

M
Marinate, meander, melt, moisten, moisturize

O
Ooze, overrun

P
Penetrate, percolate, permeate, perspire, plunge, pound, pour

R
Rise, roar, roil, roll, row, run, rush

S
Sail, saturate, scald, scull, seep, seethe, shimmer, shoot, sizzle, slabber, slap, slaver, slobber, slop, slosh, smother, snake, soak, sog, sop, souse, sparkle, spill, spin, spit, sploosh, splosh, spout, spray, spread, sprinkle, spurt, squirt, stain, steam, steep, stir, streak, submerge, submerse, suffuse, swab, sweat, sweep, swell, swim, swirl, swish

T
Thin, thread, threaten, tickle, topple, tug, tumble, twist, twizzle

U
Undulate

<u>W</u>
Wander, wash, waterlog, weep, wet, whip, whirl, wind

Nouns

<u>A</u>
Aqueduct, arroyo

<u>B</u>
Basin, bath, bay, bayou, beach, bead, beck, bog, bottleneck, bowl, brook, bubble

<u>C</u>
Canal, cascade, channel, clamminess, closeness, coast, coastline, condensation, conduit, cove, creek, current

<u>D</u>
Dam, dampness, dankness, deluge, depression, dew, dip, discharge, ditch, drib, dribble, drip, drizzle, drop, droplet, duct, dyke

<u>E</u>
Eddy, estuary, everglade

<u>F</u>
Fen, firth, flood, floodplain, flow, flux, foam, fog, froth

<u>G</u>
Globule, gulf, gully, gutter

<u>H</u>
Harbor, hollow, humidity

<u>I</u>
Inlet

<u>J</u>
Jet

<u>K</u>
Key

L
Ladle, lake, leak, liquid, logjam, lowland

M
Maelstrom, marsh, marshland, mist, moisture

O
Oar, ocean, outlet, overflow

P
Paddle, passage, pearl, peat bog, percolation, pool, port, precipitation, puddle

Q
Quagmire

R
Rain, raindrops, rainwater, reservoir, rinse, ripple, river, rivulet

S
Sea, seawall, shore, shoreline, shower, sleet, sluice, snow, snowmelt, sogginess, splash, splatter, strait, stream, surf, swamp

T
Tank, tears, tide, torrent, trench, trickle, trough, tub

U
Undercurrent, undulation

V
Vessel, vortex

W
Wake, water, water table, watercourse, watershed, waterspout, waterway, waterworks, wave, well, wetlands, wetness, whirlpool

Wind Words

Environmental ambience adds depth to writing.

Do you take advantage of it?

The opening paragraph of Edward Bulwer-Lytton's novel *Paul Clifford* reads in part:

"It was a dark and stormy night; the rain fell in torrents, except at occasional intervals, when it was checked by a violent gust of wind which swept up the streets ... rattling along the house-tops, and fiercely agitating the scanty flame of the lamps that struggled against the darkness."

Lytton's words provide an atmosphere unlike what you'd expect on a sunny day. The chapter progresses, painting a desolate word-picture of a man searching for something in the gloom. The weather infuses the opening with emotion—a premonition that unpleasant events are about to unfold.

Beware overplaying the weather card, though. Readers will lose interest, especially if you rely on words they don't understand.

Review and compare the following passages.

Danny wasn't looking forward to the suspension of door-to-door delivery. He had been a mail carrier for almost forty years, and he enjoyed his job.

This passage is pure *tell*. Although you might want to write something similar for micro fiction, the paragraph reads like a laundry list.

Almost forty years as a mail carrier, and now the big dogs at the top of the food chain intended to suspend door-to-door delivery. No more sunny days with a gentle wind in Danny's face, the tantalizing aromas from the corner bakery wafting into his nostrils. Heck, he'd even miss the wet-dog smell on rainy days when the wind drove rain into every crevice and crack.

The second paragraph dips into *show*, referring to management in a deprecatory fashion and contrasting Danny's pleasant days with the not so pleasant by inclusion of wind and how it affects him.

North, south, east, or west. Which way should she go? Cassandra crouched inside the garage until the drones were gone.

How does Cassandra know the drones are gone? Although the paragraph does provide some suspense, it could improve.

North, south, east, or west. Which way should she flee? Cassandra crouched inside the drafty garage, shivering in her scanty rags, waiting, listening. The wind wailed outside, almost drowning the whirr of the search drones. She waited until all she could hear was a gentle breeze coaxing snow through the crack beneath the door.

The words *flee* and *search* add detail. Now we know Cassandra isn't playing a game with neighborhood kids. The wind wails when she's in danger and turns into a gentle breeze after the peril disappears.

Examples you can grab as story prompts.

Note how weather augments each of the following, providing a backdrop that steers readers toward an emotional response.

The fangs of the wind ripped at Wendell's cloak. He braced against the onslaught, shouldering into the storm with fierce determination. Nothing would dissuade him from the grim task awaiting him this evil night.

A few key words, *fangs, ripped, onslaught, grim,* and *evil,* show that something unpleasant is afoot.

Puffy clouds—cotton balls in a blue sky filled with hope and cheer— billowed in the wind. Roxanne banked her anti-grav unit left at Causeway H-40.

She cursed.

This scene starts optimistic with words such as *puffy, cotton balls, blue sky, hope,* and *cheer.* We see a happy Roxanne.

Then she curses. Why? Does she collide with another anti-grav? Encounter a traffic jam? See someone she doesn't expect or want to see? Could you precede her curse with a thunderclap? A gale that steers her off course? The sight of a twister in the distance?

A ruthless gale hammered at the cliffs and churned the sea into a narrow channel. One bedraggled sail peeked out through a valley between two mountainous waves.

The grizzled lighthouse keeper bowed his head in silent prayer.

This excerpt bestows personality on the wind with *ruthless*, and likewise on the sail with *peeked*. Can you see the churning sea and bedraggled sail?

Adjectives to describe wind.

A
Aggressive, alee, aweather, angry, Arctic, arid

B
Biting, bitter, bleak, blustery, boisterous, bracing, breezy, brisk, brutal, brutish

C
Carefree, ceaseless, chilly, churning, constant, continual, cruel, cutting

D
Damp, darting, driving, dry, dusty

E
East, easterly, energizing, evil, exhilarating

F
Fair, feeble, feral, ferocious, fierce, foul, freezing

G
Gale-force, gentle, gusty

H
Harsh, high-pitched, hissing, hostile, hot, howling

I
Icy, inexorable, inhospitable, inhumane, intense, intermittent, invigorating

K
Keen, keening

L
Light, lively

M
Merciless, mighty, moaning, moist, murmuring

N
Nasty, never-ending, nippy, north, northerly

O
Offshore

P
Parching, penetrating, perpetual, persistent, piercing, potent, powerful, probing

Q
Quiet

R
Raging, raw, refreshing, relentless, remorseless, robust, roiling, ruthless

S
Sandy, savage, scorching, severe, sharp, shrill, sighing, slight, smoggy, smoky, soft, sooty, south, southerly, spirited, squally, steady, stiff, stimulating, stinging, sudden

T
Turbulent

U
Unexpected, unrelenting, untamed

V
Vicious, vigorous, violent

W
Wailing, weeping, west, westerly, wet, whipping, whispering, whistling, wild, wintry

Z
Zesty

Verbs that show wind movement and activity.

A
Assail, assault, attack

B
Batter, beat, billow, bite, blast, blow, bluster, breathe, burst

C
Carry, caterwaul, channel, chill, churn, creep

D
Damage, drift, drive, drone

E
Eddy, erode

F
Fan, flagellate, flay, fling, float, flog, flow, force, freeze

G
Gasp, glide, grab, gust

H
Hammer, harangue, huff, hurl

I
Impel

J
Judder

K
Keen

L
Lambaste, lament, lash

M
Melt, moan, murmur

O
Overcome

P
Pound, propel, puff, pummel, punish, push

R
Rage, rattle, roar, rush, rustle

S
Scourge, scream, sculpt, seethe, seize, shake, shoot, shriek, sigh, sough, spin, squall, squeal, sting, stream, strike, surge, sweep, swirl, swish, swoosh

T
Take, tear at, thaw, thrash, thrust

V
Vibrate

W
Waft, wail, wander, warm, wheeze, whine, whip, whirl, whisk, whisper, whoosh, worm

Y
Yowl

Nouns that can refer to, replace, or be affected by wind.

B
Balloon, bearing, Beaufort scale, blast, blizzard, bora, breeze, bubbles, burst

C
Cape, chinook, clothesline, cloudburst, current, curtains, cyclone

D
Dandelion fluff, deluge, direction, downpour, draft, dust

E
Energy, erosion

F
Fan, fireflies, flag, flock of birds, flow, flurry, flying carpet, force, Frisbee

G
Gale, generation, generator, glider, gnats, grit, gust

H
Hail, hailstorm, hair, headwind, hot-air balloon, hurricane

K
Kite

L
Leaves

M
Might, mistral, movement

O
Onslaught

P
Paper airplane, parachute, pine needles, pinwheel, pollen, power, propeller, protection

R
Rain, resistance, rotor, rush

S
Sail, sailboat, sand, sandstorm, shawl, shear, shelter, shower, simoom, sirocco, sleet, smog, smoke, snowstorm, speed, storm, strength

T
Tailwind, tempest, thunderstorm, tornado, trade wind, turbine, twister, typhoon

U
Umbrella

V
Velocity, vigor

W
Waves, weather balloon, weather vane, whirlwind, wind tunnel, wind-chill factor, windmill, windstorm, windsurfing

Z
Zephyr

Afterword

The English language contains over one million words, and new words are created every day. In these pages I've focused on the most common repetitions and problems encountered by writers.

Did I miss something you'd like to see included in a second volume?

Please get in touch:

Author@KathySteinemann.com

P.S. If you liked this book, please remember to leave a review.

Thanks!

Kathy

About the Author

Kathy Steinemann, Grandma Birdie to her grandkids, is an award-winning author who lives in the foothills on the Alberta side of the Canadian Rocky Mountains. She has loved words for as long as she can remember, especially when the words are frightening or futuristic or funny.

Her career has taken varying directions, including positions as editor of a small-town paper, computer-network administrator, and webmaster. She has also worked on projects in commercial art and cartooning.

Kathy's Website

KathySteinemann.com

Books by Kathy Steinemann

Humor
- Nag Nag Nag: Megan and Emmett Volume I
- Rule 1: Megan and Emmett Volume II

Speculative Fiction
- Envision: Future Fiction

Multiple Genre
- Suppose: Drabbles, Flash Fiction, and Short Stories

Alternative History
- Vanguard of Hope: Sapphire Brigade Book 1
- The Doctor's Deceit: Sapphire Brigade Book 2

Nonfiction
- The Writer's Lexicon: Descriptions, Overused Words, and Taboos
- The Writer's Lexicon Volume II
- CreateSpace Graphics Primer
- IBS-IBD Fiber Charts
- The IBS Compass
- Practical and Effective Tips for Learning Foreign Languages
- Top Tips for Packing Your Suitcase
- Top Tips for Travel by Air

Multilingual
- Life, Death and Consequences
- Leben, Tod und Konsequenzen (German Edition)
- Matthew and the Pesky Ants
- Matthias und die verflixten Ameisen (German Edition)